KU-692-228

POSITIVELY SINGLE
The Art of Being Single & Happy

Vera Peiffer was born near Cologne in Germany. At University she studied German and English Literature and Linguistics, and in 1981 she moved to Britain where she obtained a BA in Psychology. She became interested in hypnotherapy and completed a diploma at the Hypnothink Foundation, following this with further diplomas in analytical hypnotherapy at the Hypnotherapy Centre in Bournemouth and the Bill Atkinson-Ball School of Hypnotherapy.

Vera now runs a private practice as an analytical hypnotherapist/psychoanalyst in Ealing, West London. She also teaches stress management at the London Business School and is a member of the Corporation of Advanced Hypnotherapy. She is principal of The Peiffer Foundation.

By the same author

POSITIVE THINKING

STRATEGIES OF OPTIMISM

POSITIVELY SINGLE

THE ART OF BEING SINGLE & HAPPY

Vera Peiffer

ELEMENT

Shaftesbury, Dorset ● Rockport, Massachusetts
Brisbane, Queensland

© Vera Peiffer 1991

First published in Great Britain in 1991 by
Element Books Limited
Shaftesbury, Dorset SP7 8BP

Published in the USA in 1991 by
Element Books, Inc.
42 Broadway, Rockport, MA 01966

Published in Australia in 1991 by
Element Books Limited for
Jacaranda Wiley Limited
33 Park Road, Milton, Brisbane 4064

Reprinted March 1992
Reprinted February and August 1993
Reprinted 1994

First mass market paperback edition 1995

Cover design by Max Fairbrother
Typeset by Footnote Graphics, Warminster, Wiltshire
Printed and bound in Great Britain by
BPC Paperbacks Ltd, Aylesbury, Bucks.

British Library Cataloguing in Publication
data available

ISBN 1–85230–712–9

For Bernadette Ceschi a Santa Croce

CONTENTS

Happiness is the endowment with value
of all the things you have.

MILTON ERICKSON

PREFACE

SHORTLY before I began writing this book, I started going out with someone after having been single for a couple of years. Of course I was very happy. The relationship seemed very good in many respects, and I laughingly told my friends that I would now have to write *Positively Single* from memory . . .

But it was not to be. Five months later the relationship came to an end, just when, ironically, a book of mine called *How to Cope with Splitting Up* was published. Despite my upset about the break-up, I had to laugh.

So, you see, this book is written from first hand experience after all. And it is not just my own experience. In the course of compiling information for *Positively Single*, I interviewed men and women who have been without a partner for at least six months, as well as using case studies from my practice as an analytical hypnotherapist. The aim of these interviews was to find out about the main problem areas encountered by single people and to show ways of overcoming these difficulties.

In addition, the book gives examples of people who consider themselves happy singles. I was interested in finding out from them why they thought they were contented with being single and which qualities and skills they felt they possessed that made them successful. The results of these interviews can be found in Chapter 7.

You don't have to be a 'natural' from day one. We all have the ability to learn new skills and improve our outlook on life and on ourselves. We can all achieve happiness for ourselves, provided we are willing to put some work into it. If only one other person in the world can do it, you can do it too.

Vera Peiffer

1. To Be Or Not To Be . . .

THANK heaven the days are over when you were a social misfit if you were not married! These days it is acceptable for an unmarried couple to live together or even to have separate homes. As long as you are *seen* to have a partner, no one will bat an eyelid if you live 'in sin'. However, you are likely to create widespread concern amongst relatives and neighbours if you are spotted traipsing off to the cinema on your own too often.

Single men tend to arouse maternal instincts in female friends because a man on his own is considered to be helpless as a baby and therefore in urgent need of attention. Little wonder that by the time all his washing and cooking and ironing have been done for him he is *indeed* comparatively incompetent at looking after himself.

A single woman, on the other hand, does not usually attract this sort of attention because by the time she leaves the parental home she is supposed to have learned all the necessary survival skills for the outside world. Instead, she is scrutinized very carefully for any hidden flaws; and she must have some, because otherwise why would she still be single?

What most people forget is that, in nearly everyone's life, there are times when you are on your own, whether you plan it or not. Whether you have just split up with your last partner and haven't found anyone else yet, or whether your husband or wife died and left you widowed; whether you are too busy building your career or whether you simply have not yet met the right person, it is very likely that there will be certain times during your life when you are by yourself. You may even have made a conscious decision to stay single. But whatever the reason, the fact remains that you need a set of special skills to live life on your own.

The purpose of this book, therefore, is not to assess whether or not it is a good thing to be single. Equally, I have no intention of advocating either being involved in a relationship or being single. Being single is neither good nor bad, it is simply a specific state of affairs, just as is sharing your life with someone else. However, just as having a partner is not necessarily a guarantee for happiness, neither is being single necessarily a recipe for disaster. There are as many problems associated with being in a relationship as there are problems in being on your own.

However, from my professional experience, it appears that the majority of people find it harder to be on their own. Many people would rather stay in an unsatisfactory relationship than walk away and live life on their own.

Even though it has now become socially acceptable to be solo, emotionally it still appears to be a major stumbling block. Deep down inside, the idea still reigns that without a partner you are not a whole person and that your happiness ultimately depends on that one special person in your life. And yet, if you are honest, you will have to admit that you have also spent lonely moments lying in bed next to your partner.

No matter whether we are in a relationship or not, we still have to work at achieving happiness. It is foolhardy to rely on another person to provide a meaning for our life, because this other person may not be with us forever. Self-development is therefore extremely important, and being on your own can provide you with an ideal opportunity to try out new things and to learn new skills. As we become more competent at living our life, we feel better within ourselves and about ourselves, and this in turn makes us more attractive to others.

Being on your own, if only for a short time, is an opportunity you should try to make the most of because it offers a chance to widen your horizons and be your own person. This will prove to be an asset, whether you stay single or go into a relationship later on. You always have a choice between activity and passivity, happiness and unhappiness. It is really and truly up to you to make the most of your life and become *positively single*.

2. WHY ARE YOU SINGLE?

BASICALLY, there are two groups of singles: those who want to be solo, and those who don't. Neither of these groups is necessarily always that clear about their intentions, and no doubt there is always a certain degree of ambiguity, but it is probably possible to fit most people into either the 'voluntary' or the 'involuntary' category.

It may seem superfluous to include the voluntary singles in this book, because, after all, they choose their status deliberately, which suggests that they are happier single than in a relationship. This, however, is not necessarily the case, as choosing to be on your own can be (but doesn't have to be) a way of opting out. If you can't cope with relationships you may want to withdraw and simply refuse to try again. This, however, is not a very constructive way of dealing with a problem. It is like saying 'I can't have it, therefore I don't want it', and settling for second best. The problem with this approach is that you can't deny your own needs for very long without suffering the consequences. There is no point pretending that you have given up on intimate relationships when they are constantly on your mind.

People who have experienced a traumatic break-up often switch into this sour-grapes mode for a while, only to find that it does not make them any happier and that it certainly does not reflect their real feelings. If you force yourself to be single you will eventually pay the price for it. You can get bitter and hard and deprive yourself of the possibility of the warmth and closeness of genuine companionship.

This is not to say that there are not genuine voluntary singles. Deciding to go solo for a while can be a carefully considered option which you choose to take in order to have time to yourself and to sort out your life. In this context it can be very helpful to be alone to allow yourself to think things through more independently. Even though this process may continue for some time, these people tend naturally to open up to relationships after a while; in other words, they are not fanatical about being single, but at the same time they are not desperately searching for a relationship either. This, of course, is the ideal – to be equally happy on your own or with a partner.

Unfortunately, most single people come under the 'involuntary' category of soloists who find it difficult to cope with life on their own. In the same way as the sour-grapes singles use bachelorhood as a refuge, involuntary singles see relationships as a sanctuary which enables them to escape the risks which they feel a life on their own would entail. Needless to say, this is hardly a good starting point for a relationship, as these relationship-addicts are just using their partners to avoid taking responsibility for their own contentment and well-being. Instead, they place that burden on their partner who is then the automatic culprit when things go wrong.

In the rest of this chapter, I will discuss circumstances which can lead to your being left without a partner, and I will be looking at both accidental and intentional situations where this can occur.

THE YOUNG SINGLE

The period between mid-teens and mid-twenties is a very important one. During these years, young people are under great social pressure to conform to their peer group. Even though we retain this tendency to go along with the crowd later on in life, it usually wears off over the years as we gain more confidence and greater independence. During puberty and early adolescence, however, it is particularly important to be seen to be with the in-crowd, and one of the requirements for being accepted is to have a boyfriend or a girlfriend. This, of course, leaves youngsters who are without a partner high and dry.

Going out with someone is one of the first serious steps towards leaving home. As you attach yourself to a person who is not part of your family, you loosen the ties that bind you to home. Even though you still need your parents and their support, your priorities change towards the outside person, and this prepares you for eventually building your own family.

The teenage years are very complex and often confusing to young people, with physical changes and sexual desires emerging. As the youngster's appearance begins increasingly to resemble that of an adult, his or her social behaviour has to change with it, and part of that social etiquette is finding a good way to attract a girl or boy they like. Some youngsters have a personality that enables them to do so relatively easily. They have no problems hiding their self-doubts under a confident manner and are accordingly successful at finding a partner. Others, however, find this much more difficult. Shyness, coupled with self-doubt and a lack of social graces, can result in isolation, and failure to attract attention from the opposite sex will only reinforce that sense of inadequacy. The only answer might seem to be deep involvement in studies, but this cannot really make up for the fact that the youngster has not managed to find a girl- or boyfriend. This sense of failure then has an unfortunate knock-on effect in that it makes the young person feel even more awkward and thus dissuades him or her from trying again.

The situation often resolves itself at some point when the youngster changes schools or goes on to university and consequently gets in with a different crowd of people. This usually proves a golden opportunity to start again and be 'someone else'. As no one knows they are inexperienced and shy, they can turn over a new leaf. After all, they might just be coming out of a relationship for all their new mates know. . . .

It is generally true to say that the partnership issue gets hyped-up and blown out of proportion within this age group. Sexual experiences are often invented to impress friends, which in turn put those without partners under even greater pressure. In the end, anyone who doesn't have the nerve to 'invent' something feels left out.

As peer group pressure, whether real or imagined, is particularly strong during the teens and early twenties, being solo during that period is especially hard. However, inexperience is no sin, and as long as there is an ability to make friends, there is the inherent possibility of finding a partner. Manners can be improved, social skills can be learned, and if you are prepared to work on yourself you will eventually find a partner and enjoy yourself while you are on your own.

DIVORCED

During the actual process of divorce, most people are too busy to start worrying about what is going to happen when they are finally separated from their partner. The emotional and practical problems that arise during this period keep your mind occupied while you are dividing up possessions, moving out, telling friends and relatives about the break-up and generally trying to come to terms with your changed circumstances.

When children are involved, it can make the separation both easier and more difficult. On the one hand, children can be a distraction, so that if you are the one who is looking after them you initially don't have time to contemplate your own fate. As children need a lot of attention for a long time after the break-up, you might feel that your own needs have to take a back seat for a while.

On the other hand, there comes a time when it hits home that you are alone. Not only are you on your own with any problems concerning children, money, decision-making, holidays and entertainment generally, you also become painfully aware that you are not exactly footloose and fancy free as a single parent. Who will want someone with children? Is there ever going to be another partner?

If you are the one who has left the marital home, you may find yourself living in a strange place or, if you can't find a new place straight away, living with friends. You are away from your old territory and out of your old routines. At the same time, you still have to hold down a job, keep in touch with your spouse to finalize details about the divorce and you may also want to stay in touch with your children.

In a way, children can make it more difficult to get over the break-up because they constitute a powerful link between your old life and your new life as a single person, so that you cannot really ever let go of the past entirely. This can be a problem, especially if the divorce was acrimonious and the only access to the children is via your ex-partner whom you don't really wish to see any more. So even if you are the one who has left the marital home and the children, you cannot truly be an unattached person, at least not in the emotional sense of the word.

Realistically, though, it has to be said that with many couples there is also a sense of relief when they are finally out of the relationship, whether there are children or not.

Being on your own after a divorce is strange because you know that there is someone with whom you were together in the past who now lives somewhere else, and you are aware of the possibility of seeing this person again in the future. Consequently, whenever you feel lonely or desperate for companionship you begin to think about him or her and all the good times you had together, and you begin to wonder why you were unable to hold the marriage together.

These thoughts usually bring up a whole array of mixed feelings. You go over old memories and get angry at your partner for the things he or she did, and you also feel guilty about some of your own shortcomings and mistakes. The worst feeling, however, is that of loss of self-confidence. If you were the one who was left behind you begin to wonder whether there is something wrong with you. Maybe if you were more intelligent or sexier or more interesting, your partner would not have left you? These self-doubts are particularly powerful when the spouse has left you for someone else.

Even when you are the one who initiated the divorce, you can be plagued by feelings of inadequacy. Maybe you just cannot see things through? Maybe you give up too easily? Maybe you are just a failure when it comes to relationships?

To end the agony, the search starts for a replacement partner, because if you can find someone else, that must mean that you are a worthwhile person. If you can prove to yourself that someone else wants you, you are reassured that there is nothing wrong with you after all. So off you go, hunting far and wide for someone else, because there is one thing that must not be allowed to happen under *any* circumstances – you must not be on your own.

As these relationships on the rebound are mainly designed to bolster the brittle ego of the involuntary soloist, they are rarely successful. The choice of partner is made for comfort, not for compatibility, and this is why these particular relationships are more prone to be ill-matched than relationships made from free choice. Either the new partner discovers that they are just being used to fill a gap, or the divorcee is so shellshocked from their last relationship that he or she doesn't want to make any serious commitment for the time being, and so just wanders from one partner to the next in search of bouts of intimacy that will help them cope with the empty feelings.

However, this option is not open to everyone. Depending on your personality, you may feel unable to contemplate another relationship, be it serious or casual, for a while. Some people feel they need to withdraw from the outside world as they recover from their divorce. They will only see close friends occasionally and refuse to join any social activities because they feel too depressed even to consider going out.

Neither withdrawing from the world nor chasing after a new relationship is really a satisfactory solution to the fact that you now find yourself on your own. They are understandable reactions in the short term and form part of the grieving process which is necessary to work through the old relationship emotionally, but if they extend over years they can become destructive. Eventually you need to rediscover happiness and a sense of contentment. A relaxed frame of mind is a necessary attribute if you want to build a serious relationship with anyone else in the future, and the time on your own is very useful in that it allows you to work through the past constructively and then be truly free for a new relationship.

WIDOWED

There are many parallels between being divorced and being widowed, ranging from practical aspects such as the necessity to make your own decisions to the emotional problems of grief, loss of purpose in life and feelings of anger at having been 'left' by your partner. The stresses of the situation are such that the bereaved partner feels under enormous pressure, brought on by the sudden change in circumstances. It is as though your whole world has turned upside down, as though the future has suddenly disappeared through a big hole in the ground, and there is virtually nothing to live for. Often, it is only the existence of children that preserves the parent's will to live.

Grieving, just like any process of separation, goes on over a long period of time, way beyond the actual event, and way beyond an outsider's perception of what one assumes is an 'appropriate' grieving period. It is commonly expected that you should be over the loss after about a year's time, but this is a considerable underestimation of what is happening within the distressed person.

Psychologically, everyone has their own way of dealing with loss, and therefore there are variations in the length of time it takes the individual to get over the death of a partner. If the relationship has not been very close it can make it easier to recover from the loss, but this is not always the case. Even with unsatisfactory relationships, there is still a tendency to deplore the absence of the partner, despite feelings of relief which may occur at the same time.

A similar duality occurs in relationships that were happy and intimate – besides feelings of sadness there are also feelings of anger. It is almost as though the mind needs to counterbalance the stresses of grief by letting off steam through irritable thoughts, even though they seemingly contradict the positive feelings for the deceased. Unless the surviving partner is aware of the fact that this anger occurs naturally as part of the grieving process, they may find themselves with the additional problem of guilt and thinking ill of their spouse. This can easily result in a vicious circle where depression is exacerbated by guilt.

Just like divorce, bereavement has a fundamental influence on your life in that it changes your perspectives and attitudes, sometimes to a considerable extent. Even though your partner may have been ill for a long time, death still comes as a shock when it happens; and even though you know it has happened, it does not become real until some time later. There are still times when you want to rush into the study to tell him something, or when you look at the bathroom door, expecting her to come out any minute – until you suddenly realize, again, that the other person is no longer there.

We can never know how much time we will have with our partner. Accidents and illnesses happen. Fate does not distinguish between the young and the old. But whereas a younger person still stands a change of finding a new partner, elderly people may be less fortunate. For one thing, there is a greater number of women than men over the age of sixty-five which means that the ratio is unfavourable to women. Also, the older bereaved person may be less willing to take on another relationship commitment. By this age, routines have become so well established that adjustment to someone else's routine may seem impossible.

This is, however, not just a problem of old age. Even with young people, and especially people who have been single for a long time, the transition from their old living pattern to a negotiated new pattern with a partner can prove to be a stumbling block, at least in the beginning.

Once new mutual habits have been settled, life proceeds more smoothly, and it finally seems as if things had never been different.

In the meantime, however, you don't know what the future will bring. Divorced, widowed, or any other way of being an involuntary single carries with it negative emotional baggage which makes this phase of your life difficult. Pessimism sets in ('I'll *never* find another partner *ever* again!'), and the present state of affairs is looked on as a permanent institution, which translates into eternal unhappiness and loneliness for the person concerned.

We find it hard to understand the changing nature of life. When we are going through hard times, it seems that we will never be happy again, just as during times of great happiness we tend to forget the hard times as though they had never happened. The stronger the emotions that are involved, the more we get 'stuck' in the mood we are in at the time, be it good or bad.

When we have lost our partner, we need to go through a grieving process. This is necessary; it is a natural emotional process to work through the event in order to come to terms with it. You have no choice but to undergo this process, but you do have a choice when it comes to the manner in which you cope with being on your own. Rather than worrying about your unaccustomed single status, you can actively do things to make your life easier. Being widowed is an unusual situation for you right now, but so was being married at first, wasn't it? You adjusted to your new way of life then, and you can do so again. As you are beginning to get used to life by yourself, you will discover that it also has its advantages.

Many of our fears arise from ignorance about our own potential. It is not until we are forced to change that we discover what resources we have in us. This book will help you discover your hidden emotional reserves which you can learn to activate to help you cope constructively with your altered circumstances.

SINGLE BY CHOICE

Just as some people find it hard to believe that anyone could choose a life on their own, so others cannot understand why anyone would want to restrict their freedom by sharing their life with someone else. As mentioned earlier, this book is not concerned with attributing any particular virtues to either status. Whether you want to live on your own or with a partner will always have to be a personal decision and will therefore be a reflection of your personality and your particular needs at the time. You may find that these needs change after a while; there is nothing wrong with that. What is appropriate at one stage in your life may no longer be appropriate a couple of years later. It is essential to stay flexible and not block your own progress by setting rigid rules. As circumstances change, so your life changes, and your decisions may have to reflect the new situation.

As outlined previously, there are times when it can be advisable to stay single. When you have just lost your partner through divorce or death, you need time to come to terms with your loss. At this stage, you are too tied up emotionally to be ready for another serious relationship. This does not mean that you should withdraw from others. On the contrary, you will need all the support you can get from friends. You will need to be able to lean on others. This, however, is not the best state of mind in which to enter a new relationship because you have to be able to give as well as take, and at that point in time you won't be able to do a lot of giving.

Some people decide to stay solo after having gone through a number of unsuccessful relationships and use their single status as a protective shield against further failure. The idea behind this decision is that if you stay away from relationships you cannot get hurt.

Although this looks like a voluntary act, it is not really a free choice. The inability to choose the right partner or to cope with difficulties within the partnership leaves you with feelings of frustration, so you opt out, and the only other option appears to be to remain solo. What people tend to overlook, though, is the third possibility of working on the difficulties you have and finding out how this pattern of repeated failure arose in the first place. If you always go for the wrong type of person, surely the problem must also partly lie with yourself!

Once again, while you are sorting yourself out, it can be an advantage to be on your own. The important point to note in this context is that it is all right to withdraw from relationships, *as long as you use your time constructively*. If you just pull out and sulk, you are not achieving anything. If you are unhappy with the way things are, you need to go out and change them or, if this cannot be done, you have to change your attitude. Both require work and personal commitment.

You can recognize a truly happy single person from the absence of fanaticism. They won't tell you that being single is the only acceptable way of living, but neither will they make out that the only salvation lies in marriage or being with someone else. They enjoy their life wholeheartedly but keep an open mind when it comes to future relationships. They realize that the grass always seems greener on the other side of the fence, so they consciously look at the advantages of singledom while they are on their own, just as they will look at the advantages of a relationship if and when they are in one. It makes a lot more sense to count the blessings that you have right now, rather than hanker after imaginary blessings you dream of attaining in a fictional relationship.

It is an illusion to think that a relationship is a ticket to happiness, and we realize this quite clearly once we are involved in one. It is as though our memory fades as soon as we are without a partner, and instead creates an illusion of bliss with the ideal partner.

Even though in theory we understand that it requires work and dedication to keep a relationship going, we never seem to be aware that it takes an equal amount of dedication to make a solo existence work out. Being on your own dictates a different set of social skills than you need as one half of a couple. Once you are aware of this you can start working on it, and only when you do this work will you succeed.

3. SOCIAL STIGMA OR NEW TREND?

IT appears that society looks more kindly on a single man than on a single woman. A man is presumed to have chosen his mode of living because he does not want to settle down yet, or maybe because he still has wild oats to sow. All this is considered very understandable and 'typically male'. It even seems to make these men more attractive to some women who admire their lifestyle for its glamour of 'Marlboro-freedom' and macho independence. The male single can bring out in many women a maternal instinct and a longing to look after him and make him settle down – preferably with them.

Single women, on the other hand, seem to have a far shorter shelf-life. Few would assume that a woman *wants* to be by herself or, like a man, *needs* the personal space of being single in order to play the field for a while. On the contrary, when a woman is solo it is still generally assumed that this is because she *cannot get* a man, and if she says she does not want one, there must be something seriously wrong with her. It appears that the image of a fulfilled female still includes the presence of a man, even today.

However, there is no doubt that there has been a shift towards greater freedom of choice when it comes to marital status. As women become more independent by earning their own income, it has become less pressing for them to find a provider. This means that women can be more discerning about the partner they choose, and also freer, from a financial point of view, to dissolve a relationship. That is probably why there seems to be a larger number than ever of single women, especially in large towns and cities.

However, life has also changed for men. They, too, have become more independent, a fact which is often overlooked. There is a new generation of men who are perfectly capable of looking after themselves, who cook, clean, buy their own clothes and furnish their own flats, and contrary to public belief, they are not all gay. Interestingly, many of these men seem miraculously to lose all these abilities again once they are in a relationship!

Professionalism is certainly one key to a wider set of options in life. To achieve independence, it helps to have either a good education or a good business sense. If neither of the two is present, it is often back to the traditional roles of mother and housewife versus husband and breadwinner or, more recently, mother and housewife with job versus husband and breadwinner. In order to enjoy freedom you have to be financially independent, and your earnings have to be somewhat above average so that something is left at the end of the month once all the bills have been paid.

Money itself may not bring happiness, but it certainly serves as a very pleasant shock absorber for the bumps in the road of life. When you feel miserable, it is so much more agreeable to treat yourself to a weekend away than having to stay at home because you cannot afford to go out. Maybe this is why the single status is widely accepted amongst the middle classes but still frowned upon amongst the working class where traditional values seem to be firmly rooted. Because of a lack of education or a lack of money for good education, there is only a limited choice of professions for working class people so that financial independence is rarely achieved, unless the individual makes specific efforts to gain access to further education. The majority of people, however, remain in their given situation in every respect, and one of the traditions is to work, get married and have children. The more people stick to that tradition, the harder it becomes to be the outsider. Marriage is born out of necessity and is consequently made into a virtue, and any offenders against tradition are viewed with suspicion.

Preserving tradition is equally important amongst the upper classes, albeit for entirely different reasons. Here, preserving of tradition has nothing to do with a lack of money. On the contrary, it becomes a duty to marry a member of the same class in order to pass on the heritage of the respective families. Children can be looked after by nannies so that the parents still retain the maximum personal and professional freedom while fulfilling their social duty to keep up tradition.

Even though there is an increased overall trend to 'go it alone' – at least during a few years of your life – the underlying tendency still seems to point towards partnership. Even though being single is now quite widely accepted, emotionally it is still felt to be second-best. Neighbours (particularly married neighbours) are still concerned about the single girl next door who is not seeing anyone; relatives worry about their boy and the fact that he hasn't got anyone to look after him. Also, single people themselves often feel envious of their married friends because they perceive them as safely settled and therefore happy.

Even though more and more people lead their lives on their own, it is still considered a deplorable existence. But is it really so deplorable? Isn't being single merely another option which has its own advantages and disadvantages, just as relationships do?

It is perfectly understandable from a biological point of view that mankind needs to form pairs, but there are times when this is not possible, where there is no partner at hand for a while. We all have a choice how we want to spend this time. We can either make the most of it, enjoy the advantages it brings and be happy, or we can deplore our fate and have a thoroughly miserable time. It is up to us.

No matter how society views the issue, there is no doubt that bachelorhood has its positive sides. These become obvious when you have just come out of an unsatisfactory relationship. Nadine explained:

'The first few months after I split up with Brian were simply bliss. It was absolutely wonderful to be able to do everything *my* way. When I was with Brian, I had to be considerate about all his little whims. He wanted the flat tidy all the time, but he never helped to keep it that way, and he always needed to have the last word when it came to decisions about things like new curtains or new pieces of furniture. If I didn't agree with his opinion he would sulk, so in the end it was easier to give in and do as he said. It is a truly liberating feeling to be able to make your own decisions again and fulfil your own wishes. I had nearly forgotten what it feels like.'

It is a pleasant feeling when you don't have to compromise over every single issue; it is gratifying to pander exclusively to your own needs. Not having to ask anyone's consent, not having to go to the theatre when you don't want to, being able to spend an entire Sunday in front of the television, all these things are possibly self-indulgent but certainly great fun. Doing things your own way is less stressful than having to adapt to someone else's wishes. Leon told me that he would find it difficult to give up this privilege:

'I came out of a long-term relationship six months ago. It all ended quite amicably, but I can really tell the difference in myself now the pressure is off. It is great to have my freedom back, to slouch around at weekends and not shave, go to football matches again and so on. I think I may have conformed a bit too much in my relationship and forgotten what it is I like and want to do. For the time being, I really enjoy this enormously, and I'm not going to give it up in a hurry!'

However, in spite of the freedom it offers, it seems that being single is still perceived as a social stigma by many. Singles are people who could not find anyone to marry them; they have been left on the shelf and people begin to wonder what is wrong with them. Maybe they are gay or lesbian? Many singles try to counteract these assumptions by dropping into the conversation stories of ex-boyfriends or ex-girlfriends or, better still, ex-spouses. It is more honourable to be divorced than never to have been married at all. Being divorced, after all, proves that at least *one* person wanted you enough to marry you, so you can't be all that unattractive!

Elizabeth is a career woman. She works for a firm of solicitors where she holds a responsible position. With a lot of energy and hard work she has now reached the top of the ladder in her profession. She is well-liked, witty and intelligent, but at the same time utterly unhappy about the fact that, at the age of 35, she is still unmarried. Even though she is capable of tackling the most difficult job situations, she feels out of her depth when it comes to socializing, particularly at parties. During our interview, she explained why:

'Parties are my worst nightmare. When I enter a room full of people, I feel like an outsider. Everyone else seems to have a partner, except me. I feel awkward speaking to other guests because I'm sure they pity me for being on my own. I know that this problem just doesn't exist as soon as I'm with a man. Being one half of a couple gives me confidence and enables me to chat easily with others, simply because I don't feel like an old spinster.'

These feelings of incompleteness and social disapproval that come out in Elizabeth's story are not unique; they are reflected in many more interviews I conducted with women.

However, there is a problem with analysing these statements in that they are not necessarily an indication of how others view the single person, but rather how the single person views him- or herself. Elizabeth assumes that others pity her, and therefore she feels like an outsider. This is not because anyone has treated her as a second-class citizen; it is because this is how she herself perceives her single status, and consequently she projects this attitude on to others.

Interestingly, this projection can also work to your advantage, provided your expectations are positive. Sonja is a good example of how a positive attitude results in a happier outlook. When I asked her how she felt about going to parties on her own, she told me:

'It has never really bothered me. It's great to be able to make up and dress up really well and then walk in there. I'm sure that the women who are there with their husbands

or boyfriends are getting a bit worried when they see me.
I'm a sort of threat to them because I'm free.'

Here, you can see quite clearly how the perspective
changes. Because Sonja *thinks* that she is regarded as
competition by the other women, she feels in a strong
position. And yet neither Elizabeth nor Sonja really *know*
what the others are thinking.

If both of them went to the same party, they would
encounter exactly the same group of people. Let us
assume that half the party guests think that a single
woman is a sorry sight, whereas the other half think that
a woman on her own is quite exciting. Despite this mix
of opinions amongst the guests, Elizabeth comes in and
acts *as if all the guests pity her*, whereas Sonja behaves *as
if all the others think she is quite special*.

Both women are convinced that they are right, but in
fact neither of them is. The only difference between the
two is that Sonja has a good time and Elizabeth a
miserable one. Doesn't it seem worth acquiring Sonja's
attitude?

Problems such as anxiety or lack of confidence are not
so much a result of society's reaction to your single status
but rather a reflection of the image you have of yourself,
and that is something you can work on.

Rather than trying to analyze what society's attitudes
are, we should employ our time by finding out what our
own perspective is. We cannot change others, we can
only change ourselves.

4. THE PITFALLS OF BEING SOLO ...

THIS chapter considers those issues that are commonly considered to be problematic to the single person, but it will also discuss the other side of the coin, wherever applicable. You see, there always is another side to a coin, whether we want to see it or not. Sometimes we are just too lazy to look for it; sometimes we are too absorbed in feelings of self-pity to think about looking for the positive sides of our situation.

It is not the circumstances themselves that decide whether we are happy or not; it is our way of perceiving these circumstances which will determine how we fare in life. When you look upon problems as challenges, you help yourself to a more realistic view of things. Situations are never only good or only bad, but usually encompass both aspects. It is really up to us which side we want to look at. Even though some of us are born with a more optimistic personality than others, we still have the power as adults to work on our attitudes and thereby achieve a more positive outlook. We always have a choice between a positive and a negative view of the world, and even if our backgrounds are such that we are handicapped by, for example, a difficult childhood or other unfavourable circumstances, we can still take the positive decision to get professional help with these problems. There is no one better suited to make you happy than you yourself, but this means that you need to take responsibility for yourself.

The following chapters consider the various issues that constitute the major problem areas during a phase without a partner. In order to overcome these problems you will have to be prepared to learn new skills and get into a new way of thinking about yourself and your situation. It is this switch from negative to positive that the next chapters will show you how to effect.

LONELINESS

There are two types of loneliness. One is that of feeling the lack of a close and meaningful relationship with other people; the other is the feeling of inner emptiness that arises from a lack of fulfilling purposes in your life. Both can be actively dealt with (see also Chapter 6).

Also known as 'Enemy Number One', the fear of loneliness is so strong in many of us that we would rather stay in a boring or unsatisfactory relationship than take the risk of exposing ourselves to the possibility of loneliness. We would rather endure loneliness within a relationship than loneliness on our own.

It is erroneous automatically to associate being single with loneliness and having a partner with a feeling of companionship. This is by no means always the case. You need to invest a relationship with commitment to make it work, and as a result you will create feelings of togetherness and happiness. Equally you need to put effort into your life on your own to make it enjoyable for yourself. First and foremost you must realize that you are worth that effort.

Being on your own is not the same thing as being lonely. Just because you don't have a partner does not mean that the rest of mankind has been wiped off the globe as well. Loneliness can be overcome, and there is no need to remain in this state, unless you cannot be bothered to change it.

Life will be a lot easier if you have kept in touch with old friends during your relationship or, in the case of never having had a partner, if you have made friends over the years. Close friendships are a source of emotional intimacy which cannot be valued highly enough. Many people keep their friendships shallow. They don't 'invest' in them because they want to reserve intimacy for 'the man' or 'the woman' in their life. This, of course, makes you vulnerable should you ever part with that special person. It also makes any times you have to spend without a partner less pleasurable.

When you are single it is important to ensure a good social life. This can be anything from seeing your friends once a week to meeting up with others every single day. You may find it is better to see friends more rather than less, but this is a matter of individual preference. You will have to find out what your personal needs are and decide on an acceptable timetable. We are perfectly capable of spending time on our own, provided we balance out the solo times with social times.

It is neither natural nor desirable to be alone all the time. We share the world with other people, and we need these other people to enable us to live a happy and fulfilled life. Out of all those who surround us, we have to choose some people who are special to us, these usually being the ones who share our views and basic principles. We tend to be attracted to them because they boost our ego and reinforce our feelings of self-esteem; unity with our friends makes us strong. These individuals who become our friends will often be able to help us, simply because they like us and wish us well, and as we perceive them as sympathetic to us we are more likely to accept the advice they offer in times of trouble.

The closer the friendship, the less likely the possibility of loneliness. Even though friendship is different from an intimate sexual relationship, it still is a relationship based on love, although this is rarely expressed as such. Friendships can last over a lifetime, and even though you may not see each other very regularly, that feeling of closeness is there immediately on meeting again. Not living in each other's pocket all the time also has the advantage that the relationship is not under the same amount of stress as a relationship where two people live together. This may be one reason why some couples decide to keep their own separate homes even though they have a committed relationship. There is also, of course, the natural need for a physical relationship, and this can be very difficult to solve. Some singles find that they are mercifully spared that problem. As one single man told me:

> 'After I split up with my girlfriend of three years, I just didn't want anyone else for a long time. I didn't have sex until four years later when I started going out with another woman.'

And a single lady who was addressed on that topic:

> 'I like sex when I'm going out with someone. When I'm solo I just don't get the desire at all.'

But alas, it doesn't work like that for everyone. People with a higher sex drive find themselves in the unenviable position of being left with the urge but without the partner. This problem, let me assure you, concerns both men *and* women and applies to people of all ages, from the twenty-year-old to the seventy-five-year-old pensioner.

The question is, what do you want to do if you find yourself in this position? Even though as a single you don't have to worry about being unfaithful to a partner, the situation is still tricky. You don't want to pick up just anyone, especially when you think about AIDS and other sex-related diseases. Sometimes, an opportunity might present itself where you encounter someone at a party or during a professional meeting which leads to a one-night-stand or even to a casual sexual relationship.

This is perfectly all right if you are both happy with the limits that a purely physical relationship imposes. Problems arise, however, if both parties start on a casual footing and then one of the two gets emotionally involved while the other partner remains uncommitted.

Some women use sex as a ploy, consciously or unconsciously, to get into a man's life, hoping that once the man gets used to them being around, he will want to commit himself, but this strategy often backfires. It appears that women have a tendency to get emotionally involved with their partner once they have had sex with him a few times, whereas men seem to be able to detach their emotions more clearly from the sexual act itself. As long as you are fully aware of all these factors as you go into a casual affair, you should not encounter any problems, provided you are not disrupting a marriage (or a similarly close relationship) with the intent of procuring the partner for yourself.

Whether you feel lonely emotionally or physically, there is nothing wrong with being sad when you are on your own. We all get these feelings of loneliness once in a while, whether we are single or in a relationship, and we have to accept these feelings. There is little point in blaming yourself when you feel depressed because it doesn't really achieve anything except add an extra problem, namely self-contempt. If you call yourself weak for having these occasional feelings of downheartedness, then you are being unfair and over-demanding towards yourself. There is nothing unnatural about sadness; it is just one of a number of emotions we all experience, and it does not imply any shortcoming in you as a person to feel it every once in a while.

Some people find it quite therapeutic to indulge in a good cry when they feel lonely; others find the feeling unpleasant and prefer to distract themselves by launching into some sort of activity. Whichever you choose for yourself, please don't forget that you are *entitled* to feel that emotion. No one is cheerful and optimistic all the time; everybody has moments of helplessness where life seems grey and unpromising; but remember – there is never a rainbow without rain. There are plenty of people who would love you to speak to them, people who can become your friends, or even lovers. If you never reach out and contact them, you will never know.

BOREDOM

In a twosome, you can often feel quite happy just being with the other person without necessarily always doing anything special. When you are on your own, however, you suddenly find that you have to make your own entertainment. Whereas before there was someone else who would go out with you and who would share your evenings and weekends, there is now a painful void.

All of a sudden, your spare time loses its appeal. Whereas before you could not wait to get home in the evenings or for your partner to come back from work, now you are beginning to dread these periods which you used to enjoy so much.

Organizing events for your free time now becomes a necessity rather than an optional extra. If you don't create some pleasurable events to look forward to, no one else will. But how is it that it seems so much easier to make such efforts when you feel you are doing it for yourself *and* for someone else, rather than arranging an event just for yourself? It is this attitude of 'Oh well, it's only me' that becomes an excuse. It is as though your own needs didn't count, as though you were not worth consideration.

This issue can become a problem, both for young people who have never had a partner and for people who have just come out of a relationship. Let's look at the former group first.

When you are at school or at college, you belong to a group of people with whom you are familiar. You know the rules of your social environment, and you are a part of it. It is likely that in such a group there are at least a few individuals who organize events or initiate some form of entertainment such as parties or interest groups, so that there are always opportunities to join in if you want to. These opportunities are not initiated by you though, they just happen to be part of the set-up. You have, therefore, only partaken in what was on offer, but perhaps you have not yet learned how to organize entertainment yourself.

People who have come out of a relationship will often face similar problems. Because there has been someone else around more or less constantly, you have set up your joint routines which have filled your time together. Now you find yourself on your own, with a routine that doesn't work any more because it was conceived for two; in other words, you are back to square one. The old pattern is disrupted, and there is no new pattern to replace it.

The hardest thing about overcoming boredom is that you need to make efforts which are often not particularly rewarding to start off with. You may have dragged yourself out of the house in order to meet up with some friends, and then you don't really enjoy the evening because you can't get involved in what is happening. You feel self-conscious and uncomfortable with the new situation and just want to leave. Then you go home and tell yourself that you will certainly not repeat *that* experiment in a hurry . . .

Or you decide to go out for the afternoon and visit an exhibition for a couple of hours. As you get there you start feeling awfully conspicuous as you are walking about, and you don't know what to do with your hands. You are not allowed to smoke and you were too stingy to buy a catalogue, so you walk through the rooms quickly, and before you know it you are at the exit. You can't really remember what you have seen and you have certainly not had a good time.

This is where many people give up. They find it either too tedious or too frightening to relieve their boredom. The amount of energy they use up in order to entertain themselves bears no relation to the pleasure they get out of their endeavours. But don't forget that you are learning a brand-new skill, so it is unlikely that you are going to get it right straight away.

Imagine if babies had your attitude! They would say, 'Oh well, I have tried a few times now to walk over to the other side of the room, but I don't seem to be able to do it without falling, so I don't think I'll bother trying again.' If they did, we would be a nation of crawlers!

Change is uncomfortable; getting into new habits feels awkward. This is normal. Keep your goal firmly in front of you, focus on the enjoyable aspects of life and keep practising; soon you will achieve your first successes. Don't let a few unsuccessful attempts stop you.

Realistically you must expect to put in a lot of work at first without getting the returns you hope for. In the short term, this can mean that you initially have a harder time than before you commenced with your efforts. However, you are not working on a short term project; you want to achieve something that you can build on in the future, a skill that will last a lifetime. You wouldn't dream of going on a diet for three days and expect to lose a stone in weight within this period. It is the same with everything else in life – you have to persevere to get results. Complaining about the injustice of life is a waste of time. It is far better to spend that time actively working on the issues that bother you (see also *Strategies of Optimism*).

Boredom is a sign that you have failed to attribute meaning to what you are doing. You do something mechanically without getting involved, and therefore it leaves you unfulfilled. Activities do not have a meaning per se, you have to give them a meaning. People vary in what they select as interesting; what is meaningful to one person may be of indifference to another. Doing the ironing usually has little meaning because it is a repetitive task that does not hold a great deal of satisfaction, whereas working in the garden is considered by many to be meaningful because it is varied and yields tangible results.

It is mostly when we experience progress in our chosen activity that we become more involved with it. The process of development itself can become the driving force behind our endeavours. As we acquire a new skill, for example learning a foreign language, we do so with a specific aim in mind. Maybe we want to be able to converse with the locals of a holiday resort we go to every year; maybe command of a new language will help us advance in our job. Learning the language is therefore directed towards a specific objective, and this gives significance and meaning to our efforts. As we get better at communicating in this language, our aim becomes more real. We can see more and more clearly how we can successfully apply what we have learned, and the more we do so the more involved we become with what we are doing.

When you are unhappy, it can be a lot harder to immerse yourself in an activity. Interruption by negative thoughts makes it difficult to concentrate on what you are doing, and this can result in feeling that you are faced with an impossible task. Don't forget, though that even a few moments of distraction are valuable. Even though you may be spending one hour walking through a gallery and only get a few moments' enjoyment out of it, you have made a start. Eventually your efforts are going to pay off, so don't give up just because things are not perfect straight away.

Involve other people in your plans. When you find your motivation flagging, it helps to have someone else to push you forward. Going out and doing things gives you something to think about and provides you with material for conversation. If you are bored you can easily become boring, and that is the last thing you want to be when you are single. Choose a few areas of interest and start filling your diary with things to do. It may look daunting, but as you get used to being more active you will feel better for it. Once you get the hang of it, you will wonder how you ever found the time to wash your socks on a Sunday!

DECISION-MAKING

Where should you go on holiday? What colour wallpaper would look good in your living-room? Should you take in a lodger? Who do you invite to your party?

In a relationship, we often rely on our partner to make these everyday decisions for us. When we are solo, we suddenly find ourselves without anyone to whom we can pass the responsibility.

There seem to be certain areas where decision-making is specifically gender-orientated. When it comes to colour schemes, household items or clothes, for example, it is mostly the women who feel competent, whereas in technical or financial matters, men seem to take the lead.

When you are on your own, you are confronted with a number of decisions which you may feel are outside your area of competence, and this can be quite a frightening experience. Sheila had been married for fifteen years when her husband Bob died of a heart attack, leaving her with two children. Having been at home since her marriage, Sheila felt completely out of her depth when she realized how many things she would have to handle which had previously been seen to by her husband. She came to see me eight months after Bob's death, explaining that she was unable to cope. She was in a state of anxiety that bordered on panic whenever the need to make a decision arose. Amidst feelings of anger at her deceased husband for having 'left' her and anger at her own inability to adapt to her new situation, she told me that she was so afraid of making a wrong decision that she preferred to avoid the issue altogether. Her self-confidence, which had never been particularly strong, began to dwindle even more as she realized she was losing control.

Her financial situation was such that it was necessary for her to find work if she wanted to continue living in her house. Even though Sheila had worked before her marriage, the prospect of going out and finding a job now after such a long break filled her with terror. Could she go back to working as a receptionist after all these years? Would she be able to understand the new systems? Maybe she was too old to learn? What if her colleagues didn't accept her? The problems surrounding a potential job seemed so complex and confusing that Sheila had not even started looking at any job advertisements. At the same time, pressure to do something was beginning to build up because money was running low.

Sheila did get a job eventually and found that even though she had to put in a lot of effort to learn about new technology, she enjoyed her work and found that it was not as difficult as she had expected.

Sheila's case is admittedly one of the more dramatic ones, but it serves to show quite clearly the predicament in which you can find yourself when faced with an unaccustomed situation. Whether you have to make up your mind about moving house or getting your overdraft facility sorted out with your bank manager, the fact remains that you will have to go through a number of steps in order to reach a decision.

You already know what those steps are when it comes to issues with which you feel familiar. You may have dealt competently with financial decisions in the past, but now that you are faced with buying a washing-machine, you can't decide whether you want one or not.

Think for a moment how you would go about making a choice in the following imaginary situation. Let us assume, for example, that you are in a position at work where you have to hire people. Before you even get anyone in for an interview, you make sure that you *specify* exactly what sort of position you want to fill. This is a process which has to be completed before you can even put an advertisement in the papers. Then you will have to vet the applications you get, *comparing* what the candidates have to offer with what you need. You will then *select* a number of possible contenders and gather more details from them in the interviews, and finally you *decide* on the person who comes closest to your requirements.

You will find that there are four distinct steps in the above. First, you specify your needs, then you compare your options, then you whittle down those options to a few favourites and, once you have looked at those more closely, you finally decide on the one that suits you best.

Let us apply these steps to a specific example. Let us assume that you have finally decided to pep up your social life and ask a few people around for dinner. You have never organized anything like this before because this was always your girlfriend's domain. The whole enterprise looks rather daunting to you as you start thinking about it. Who should you ask? Should you make it a formal or informal affair?

First of all, sit down and relax for a moment. Are you serious about your idea? Then get a piece of paper and a pen. Before you start writing down anything, close your eyes for a moment and try out a few mental images. Visualize a formal dinner party with people sitting around a table. Now imagine an informal one with people helping themselves from a buffet. Visualize a small number of people, then lots of people. What are the pictures that come to your mind? Select the one that creates the most pleasant feelings as you imagine it.

Let us say you have decided to have an informal get-together for a small number of people. You have now *specified* what is is you want, and this already solves one of your questions, namely whether you want a formal or an informal gathering. Now start thinking about the people that you would like to invite and jot down names on your piece of paper. *Compare* the people on your list and *select* the ones that you think would be most likely to fit into your concept of a relaxed get-together. Check through your selection one more time and you will have made your *decision* about who to invite.

Any decision is as good as its initial specification. Be clear about what it is you want, and be sure to choose what *you* would like to happen. As the organizer who has to do all the work, you might as well make it into an occasion that you enjoy. A lot of valuable energy is squandered by trying to guess what other people want and making decisions that are based on assumptions about what would please others. The problem with this approach is that you are trying to be someone you are not, and doing that means neglecting your own needs.

But what if you feel unable to make even the initial specification? Some subject areas might appear so alien that it seems foolhardy to try and sort them out by yourself. Karen told me:

> 'While Rodney was with me, he used to look after all our financial matters. Now I find that my bank account is heavily overdrawn, and I don't even know what half the deductions are for. I feel I'm in a right mess, but I'm scared of tackling this financial problem. I never had to deal with anything like this before.'

If we are not sure how to solve a problem, we often try to make it go away by ignoring it. Unfortunately, procrastination only makes matters worse, and in the end, you will have to confront the problem. You will achieve peace of mind much more quickly if you take action as soon as possible. If you don't feel competent to make a decision, consult someone who can help. Make an appointment with your bank manager or ask a friend to help you sort matters out. The less you understand your problem, the more threatening it looks. Once you understand what your position is, you can compare and then select your options, with or without help from someone else.

Another person may even be able to make that final decision for you, but please be aware that in the end, the responsibility for your choice lies with you. This may well mean that every once in a while you find that you have selected an option which isn't ideal, but it is impossible to get everything right all the time.

You are making a decision even when you refuse to make up your mind, so you may as well be active in the process. As you take responsibility for your choices, you gain more control over your life, and you will feel better for it.

SOCIAL LIFE

If you hate parties, can you still have a good social life? Of course you can! Just because you don't rush from one festivity to the next does not mean that you are a social failure. There are a great many opportunities to be in contact with other people by going to classes, clubs, interest groups and other social gatherings where people share your interests.

We all have different needs when it comes to socializing. Some of us are quite happy in small groups or on a one-to-one basis; others need events that involve larger crowds. Whether the event is a dinner party or a pub crawl, the emphasis is on the people component. It is the social contact with others that counts.

Establishing this contact can seem difficult, however. It is not an uncommon thing for singles to reject offers of going out with friends simply because that would be second-best to going out with a partner. Or if they do go along, they have already made up their mind that they cannot possibly have a good time.

Remember Elizabeth in Chapter 3? She felt gauche and tongue-tied going to parties on her own, whereas Sonja felt that she attracted positive attention as a single woman. Both women were intelligent, attractive and witty. They both had highpowered jobs and could hold an interesting conversation, but one of them felt good and the other one felt bad about herself.

The only thing that counts is the attitude of the individual herself, and this then works as a self-fulfilling prophecy – you act according to your beliefs. In Elizabeth's case, a situation was created where she walked into a party looking and behaving in a subdued way. Other people picked up these signals subconsciously or consciously and treated her accordingly. They judged her as a nice person but somewhat lack-lustre, which in turn confirmed her belief that others pitied her, and the whole experience turned into a vicious circle that made her even more reluctant to go to the next party by herself.

This, of course, also works the other way round. With a positive attitude, your self-esteem radiates around you and attracts others which in turn reinforces your self-confidence and makes you look forward to the next social occasion.

The importance of having a good social life as a single it that it helps you keep a more balanced perspective on life. Being absorbed in yourself for long periods of time makes for a rigid outlook. We need other people to help us re-assess our opinions and attitudes or we go stale and get locked into the same old routines.

However, other people may not always share our views, and this can make us feel uncomfortable. We can avoid that risk by addressing only 'safe' topics in conversations and by not being too specific about what we really think. This is why talking about the weather is such a popular opener during a first encounter. You can safely comment on it without giving anything away. Other small talk openers include sports events, property prices, the educational system and even current politics to a certain extent. These topics are sufficient to keep a conversation going and can often be quite interesting, but they stay very much at the shallow end of communication. They are useful in that they provide a starting point which helps you get to know the other person by watching how they speak, their gestures and body language, facial expressions and so on. However, we all know how a person can appear to be, for example, confident on the outside, whereas when we get to know them better we find that they are quite unsure of themselves. So when we engage in small talk with someone we have to be aware of these limitations.

If your social life consists of these pleasant, albeit

superficial, types of encounter, they will help you while away time, but they are hardly fulfilling. On the whole, men seem to find it more difficult than women to get past this first stage of communication. Once you feel your partner in conversation is on your wavelength, you have the option of being more open about yourself, and this is where women seem to be more willing to take a risk than men. Although attitudes are changing, there is still a great reluctance in many men to talk about their feelings. A few of the men I interviewed said that they were able to talk about personal issues with women but were unable to do so with male friends because they were afraid of losing face. Men have obviously become more aware of their emotions, but the old rules still apply, namely that it is a weakness for a man to talk about feelings to other men. So instead, they talk shop, or discuss the Cup Final. . . .

As long as you can speak to *someone* about your feelings, as long as there is at least one outlet for emotions, you are reasonably all right. Usually, it is your partner who will fulfil that function.

Life becomes a lot more difficult if you are solo, especially if you have not learned to open up to others and to keep friendships going. In order to lead a fulfilled life as a single, you will need one or two of these close friendships so that you are provided with an emotional basis from which you can operate.

David is divorced, without children, and has been single for two years. After selling the marital home he moved into his own flat.

'When I first moved out I just couldn't cope. I started drinking far too much and neglected my job, but I was lucky to have this friend from university who pulled me through. He sat and listened to me for hours and helped me put things into perspective again. It was then that I realized how important it is to have friends that you can talk to. I have learned to talk about my feelings a lot more through this experience, and I wonder whether Karen would still be with me had I been able to be more open in my marriage . . . Anyway, now that I've started talking I find it much easier to understand other people and why they act as they do. It's really quite interesting.'

The value of close friendships was emphasized by many of the singles interviewed. Christine explained her point of view as follows:

> 'I quite enjoy being single. It has its definite advantages over living with someone. Yes, of course, it also has its drawbacks, but I think I'm coping with those reasonably well. Mind you, I don't think I could be as happy as I am without my friends; in fact, they are incredibly important. You just need to have people that you can feel close to, and I couldn't do without them. I need that closeness or I'd be really lonely.'

It is not necessarily the person with the most entries in their diary who is the happiest. It is not quantity that matters but quality. Superficial social interaction is fine, as long as there is also some deeper level of companionship in your life.

Later in the book I will go into more detail about how to make friends and how to maintain friendships (see Chapter 6). These are important skills to learn, and they will also prove useful should you go into another relationship. There are many rules that apply both to friendships and more intimate relationships.

Your social life needs more attention when you are single than when you are in a relationship. Contacts with other people are essential to keep a sound balance between solitude and company, and it is worth giving this aspect of your life a great deal of thought.

There may be a temptation to neglect your needs for companionship, and paradoxically this often happens when you need others most. When things have gone wrong in your life and when you feel depressed, you tend to withdraw and hide from the world. This is all right for a while, but you may find that you have lost touch with the outside world once you feel better again, and it can feel awkward taking the initiative and going out again. Will your friends still want to see you? Will you be asked embarrassing questions about why you have not been around for a while? Will you have anything to talk about?

When your contact with the outside world has been disrupted for a while for whatever reason, these doubts can create veritable barriers to getting back into a social routine. But let me assure you that your fears are nearly always worse than reality. I will not pretend that you will drift back effortlessly into your old circle of friends or that you will find it easy to establish new friendships. What I am saying is that it is worth making the effort to overcome your apprehension and get yourself into social circulation. None of us can be alone all the time.

In the following chapters you will find practical guidelines on how to go about launching yourself into a more satisfying and fulfilled life. But don't forget – this book is only as good as the action you take to put my advice into practice! In the end, the responsibility for your happiness lies in your hands, and in your hands only.

HOLIDAYS

You can just see it, can't you? A woman on her own, sitting at a table by herself in the restaurant of her hotel, waiting to be served, uncomfortable and exposed to the view of all the other guests who seem to be there in couples or little groups. Or the man sitting at the bar of a little café at his holiday resort, drinking and smoking more than he really wants to, just to give him something to do because he feels awkward.

These are the pictures that come to most people's minds when they think about going on holiday on their own. How much easier it is to go with just *one* other person! It seems to make you automatically invisible and inconspicuous when you are in company, but the moment you leave the shelter of the group you seem to become the centre of attention and stick out of the crowd like a sore thumb. No wonder most people dread the experience and try to avoid it at all cost!

So what do you do? You have been working hard all year and you really need a holiday, but you simply can't face the stress of feeling conspicuous and uncomfortable for a couple of weeks on the Costa del Sol or in a Swiss ski resort. You like the idea of going away, but when it comes to the practical side of being there on your own, your self-confidence falters.

If you feel particularly shy about being out and about by yourself, you may want to start with an easy option. For one thing, make your holiday short. Instead of taking two weeks in a row, divide up your time into two chunks of one week each. This has the advantage of giving you several breaks during the year, and besides, if things don't work out to your satisfaction, you have only lost one week rather than two. Also, you may want to try out a number of different holiday options to see which one suits you best, and the more time slots you have available to experiment with, the sooner you will find out what type of holiday you enjoy most.

Even though it may not sound like a 'proper' holiday, you could start off by staying at home and organizing days out, with your home as a base to return to in the evenings. A good way of organizing your holiday would be to set aside a number of days to spend at home, getting jobs done that you have wanted to finish for a long time, and intersperse those duty days with days out. Please note, however, that taking a week off to decorate your flat does not qualify as a holiday – you should dedicate at least half of your time to leisure activities.

It is a good idea to plan your week systematically. Take the time to jot down a list of projects that need doing at home, for example writing letters, rearranging furniture in your sitting room or finishing that shelving system. Now draw another list of activities that take you away from home for a day, for example sightseeing in another city, visiting a friend, going for a drive in the countryside, going for a swim, going for a meal somewhere, and so on. Put down too much rather than too little on your list. Pick out the items about which you feel reasonably confident.

If you decide on going to visit another town and you need to eat out, choose a small place to start with. You will notice that you automatically go for a seat by the wall because this is less exposed than a place in the middle, so this should be another consideration when you choose a café, restaurant or pub. Having something

to do while you wait helps; you can write postcards or
letters, or you can read.

If you want to read, be clear about the signals you
send out. Reading a newspaper gives you more to do
than reading a book. You can turn a page more often
and it requires less concentration. When you read a book
you look more absorbed and studious and less relaxed.
If you are anxious to avoid people talking to you, take
a book and a pad of paper and start underlining sen-
tences and making notes. This is a sure way of signalling
to everybody around that you are busy and not open to
conversation. With a newspaper, you are more flexible.
You can finish an article and then look up and look
around you. In this manner, you can establish eye contact and indicate by smiling at someone that you are
approachable.

Books and newspapers are all items that can serve as
props to overcome initial uncomfortable feelings of sitting
somewhere on your own. Do use these props – they are
helpful and get you out of the house, and once you feel
more confident you will even be able to take in what
you are reading!

Initially, you may find that the effort of going out is
bigger than the enjoyment you get out of it, but please
don't give up. It *does* become easier as you do it more
often, and you will find that you can concentrate more
easily on the scenery around you, getting more absorbed
in what you are doing rather than constantly assessing
whether you look foolish or not.

If you find it difficult to impose a structure on your
holiday yourself, let someone else do it for you. When
you choose an activity holiday, for example, you will
find that your day is planned out to a large extent. This
can be quite pleasant, especially if you find it difficult
just to laze about. Pursuing a hobby during your vacation
is still relaxing because there is no pressure on you, even
though you might get quite carried away by what you
are doing.

When you are away from home and getting involved
in projects that differ from your everyday pursuits, you
detach yourself from work and all your old routines. This
is very important, not just to recoup strength, but also

to take a step back mentally and look at life from a different viewpoint. As long as you stay at home this is difficult, because the well-known surroundings restrict you to old ways of thinking. Moving away from home for a while has the advantage of helping you to change location *and* outlook at the same time. Once you have removed yourself from your everyday problems, things can get back into perspective; this will happen easily and effortlessly. This is why it is essential you should make sure that you go on holiday, especially when you are single. You need the distraction, just like everyone else. You deserve to have a good time, so take the trouble to find out what it is you need.

There is a vast amount of variety when it comes to activity holidays. Get all the brochures you can and sort through them quickly. Divide them up into the 'possibles' and the 'unacceptables'. It doesn't really matter what criteria you use, just go by your gut feelings to start off with. Once you have checked on the dates when you are free to go away as well as the money you can afford to spend, go through your 'possibles' again and sift out the ones that don't fit your timetable or budget. If you are left with more than one to choose from, use your imagination to help you make a decision.

Let me explain how you do this. Let us assume you are unable to decide between a painting course holiday and a cycling holiday. Sit down somewhere quietly and close your eyes. Now begin to think of the first option, creating images of yourself painting. Spend a few minutes watching yourself or feeling yourself being on that holiday and note how you *feel* as you do so. Now do the same with your second option, imagining yourself cycling along, and again, pay attention to how you feel as you go through this possibility mentally. Which option 'feels' better as you think about it? Which do you find more enjoyable to imagine? You may be surprised at what feels better as you run through your two internal films, but it makes good sense to follow that inner voice as you make your final selection. We all have a very reliable sixth sense in us, so why not use it? All you need to do is relax and listen to what is happening inside and you can't go wrong.

Activity holidays have the further advantage of making you a member of a group of people who all have a common interest, and this means that it becomes a lot easier to talk to others. Have you ever noticed how mothers with young children or people with dogs find it so easy to get chatting? It appears to be a publicly accepted, if unofficial, rule that if you share an interest or if you visibly have something in common you can address total strangers with impunity. The contact is legitimate because that person is, just like you, riding a motorbike, jogging or pushing a pram. When there are no such obvious similarities, people tend to be a lot more distrustful and unwilling to allow any advances.

It is pleasant to be a member of a group because it reinforces your enjoyment. John is quite used to going on holiday by himself, but he has one quibble with his situation.

'I am perfectly happy to go away on my own. There is just that one drawback, and that is you can't share your happiness. Last year I went to the States, and I was looking down over a bay which was teeming with dolphins. It was such a fantastic sight and I just wanted to jump up and down and say "Look! Look!", but I couldn't because there was nobody there.'

When you are in a group you are bound to find at least one or two people who are on your wavelength. All it takes is an open mind and a willingness to be approached or, even better, actively to approach others, and you will have a marvellous time.

Many of the people interviewed said that once they had made up their mind to venture out on a holiday on their own, it wasn't as bad as they had anticipated. Lydia said:

'The trick is to keep an open mind and not to expect the holiday to go in one particular way. When I first went on a holiday by myself, I had gone with the expectation of meeting new people and getting into lots of conversations while I was doing my sightseeing. When this didn't really happen after the first couple of days, I was disappointed. But then I decided to just let events take their course, and from that moment on I really started enjoying myself . . . I also found it wonderful to be able to go back to the hotel and have a nap for an hour or so if I felt like it, with no one else to consider.'

Those interviewed who found their attempt at going on a solo holiday unsuccessful were people who assessed themselves as lacking in self-confidence and social skills which made it very unsatisfactory for them when they had to rely on their own resources on holiday. All these people, however, had had a problem with their confidence when they were with a partner, so their shyness was just exacerbated when they became singles.

The basic message of this chapter is *keep trying*. You have nothing to lose and a lot to gain. It is likely that your fears are worse than the actual reality, and you may find that you surprise yourself at how well you are doing. Remember what Lydia said and just go along with whatever happens. Start on an easy project and work your way up. Hundreds of single people have done it before you and have been successful, so why not you?

FINANCES

Financial matters can be overwhelming if you are not used to dealing with them. It can be a frightening experience when you are left alone, a housewife with children and no idea how to handle money because your husband always looked after that side. You suddenly find yourself in a state of chaos, grieving, trying to comfort the children and attempting to fathom out your financial situation.

Several of the widowed women I interviewed confessed that they had never shown great interest in financial matters while their husbands were around, and when they found themselves thrown in at the deep end, they were at a loss how to deal with it. Elinor admitted that she had no idea what their monthly outgoings were:

'I didn't know what insurances Ted had paid into and whether I could claim anything off anyone. I didn't know what the direct debits were that came off our bank account, nor where to look for any of the paperwork. Somehow, I had never bothered with all that, and I resented having to concern myself with these financial matters all of a sudden. I felt angry at Ted for having dropped me in it like that and leaving me to cope with this awful situation.'

Having to deal with money matters while you are still struggling with bereavement is difficult, and matters are made worse by the fact that your mind is often over-loaded with conflicting emotions and thoughts that prevent you from thinking clearly. It is easy to start panicking when you feel that confused.

In a situation like that, it is a good idea to get outside help. There is nothing wrong with admitting that you want assistance with a problem like this. On the con-trary, it shows that you have common sense. There is no point in sticking your head in the sand and hoping that the problem will go away, because it won't. There is no point in leaving letters from the bank unopened in their envelopes; eventually the situation is going to catch up with you. It is better to take the bull by the horns and start sorting out your financial affairs. People that can help you with this include your husband's employer's accounts department which will be able to advise you what income you can expect as a widow. A friend might be able to assist you in sorting through paperwork at home to determine what items are being paid off via your bank account, whether they are loans or permanent insurance payments, and so on. If you don't have someone who can help you on a private basis, approach your bank manager and ask for advice. The sooner you know where you stand, the better.

Another group of people who seem to struggle with financial matters are those who find it difficult to monitor their spending. Overspending can be due to inexperience or to a sense of dissatisfaction with your life. When you are on your own, you can get away with it more easily because there is no one else around to ask awkward questions and thereby put the brakes on your spending sprees. It is as though you were making up for the fact that you are missing out on a relationship by treating yourself to new clothes, for example.

Another reason for overspending is, paradoxically, because you don't have any money. Rosemary said:

> 'It is really silly, but whenever I'm in financial trouble, I go and spend money. Of course, that gets me into even greater trouble and, for a while, I am sensible again and hold back because I have a guilty conscience. After that I'm OK for a while, but once I have had to pay a few big bills and my finances are difficult again, there I go again, comfort-buying!'

Credit cards constitute a major temptation in this context. It is too easy to spend and ignore the fact that you will have to pay it back in the future, and with cards being readily available, you can get into a situation where you have several store or credit cards and slowly lose sight of the total amount you have spent. People who compulsively spend money are often reluctant to look at their balance sheets. At the back of their mind they know that they have been foolish, but they don't want to be confronted with the written evidence of it.

But it is not just the big spenders who shy away from bank letters. There are also those who are simply afraid of anything to do with figures. They feel confused and unnerved by the various columns and abbreviations in their statement, and they feel reluctant to ask for an explanation because they feel they would not understand it anyway or be considered stupid for asking.

Whatever the reason for the reluctance to attend to your finances, there is no doubt that you will have to face up to them one day. Procrastination doesn't make the problem disappear, it just prolongs the agony. You may have to invest some time and effort in sorting out your affairs, but at least you will know where you stand, and this will enable you to make informed decisions when it comes to future financial decisions.

When you are on your own, it is particularly important that you should take control over what is happening in your life, and there is no way you can ignore your finances. Ultimately, you are the one who carries the responsibility for your well-being and your financial security. Learning how to deal competently with money can only be an asset to you, and it is not as difficult or complicated as you may think. You may have to iron out past mistakes, but it can be done. Take advantage of all the outside help that is available and get going!

5. ... THE TYPES WHO FALL INTO THEM ...

THERE are certain characteristics that make it difficult for someone to be solo, just as there are personality types that cope more easily. You will find some stories of successful singles in Chapter 7, but first let us look at those others who find it hard to master life on their own.

I am aware that my descriptions of various 'types' are generalizations and that their particular characteristics are exaggerated, but this is intentional. Highlighting idiosyncrasies in the various examples may turn these types into caricatures, but it also helps to illustrate more clearly the problem areas to watch out for.

For each category of people I have set two scenarios which are typical for their situation. The first describes how this type of person is perceived by the outside world, and the other shows how he or she views their life themselves. I will also briefly discuss ways of helping this particular type to deal with their problems more constructively and improve the quality of their life.

As you are reading through this chapter, hopefully you will become more aware of the attitudes and thought patterns that underlie the inability to come to terms with being single. You may recognize yourself or people you know in some of the examples, and, more likely than not, you will find that you are in fact a mixture of several different personality types. Don't worry – there is nothing wrong with you! Hardly anyone fits into one category only; we all have a variety of traits that are derived from different personality types, with one or two dominant characteristics. It is those prominent propensities that will determine what your official label will be, whether 'introvert' or 'extrovert', 'difficult' or 'easygoing', 'selfish' or 'altruistic'. However, just because you have that label does not mean that you don't have the opposite positive quality in you as well; it just means that one facet is more pronounced than the other.

There is also a difference between private life and public life. We behave differently, depending on whether we are at a party, at home or at a company function with two of our bosses present. We may present an entirely different picture on each of these occasions. Someone who is loud and boisterous at parties may be morose and depressed when they are at home, and far from happy. So let's bear in mind that outward appearances can be deceptive and that, just because someone looks or acts in an extrovert manner, they need not necessarily be happy on the inside.

But whatever the problem area, you can do something about it. Chapter 6 will give you practical advice on how to find a way out of the trap into which you have fallen, but first, let us have a look at what got you into the trap in the first place.

THE RECLUSE

Also known as The Confirmed Bachelor or The Old Girl Next Door, the recluse is someone who prefers to iron their underwear and repot their plants rather than meet up with other people.

VIEW FROM THE OUTSIDE

The recluse is rarely seen outside their home, except for the necessary outings like shopping, going to the post office or going to work. Usually in the middle-aged to retirement age bracket, the recluse has a strict routine.

A walk will always take place at the same time of day and the crossword puzzle will not be started until the washing-up has been cleared away.

On the whole, the recluse discourages unannounced visits and restricts neighbourly conversations to a brief greeting. If the milkman knocks on the door to collect his money, the recluse will open it only far enough to be able to peer out cautiously, then shut it immediately to return after a few minutes with the exact change.

However, the recluse is not necessarily unfriendly or impolite but just finds it difficult to deal with fellow human beings. The recluse feels more at ease chatting to their budgie than they do talking to their neighbour of twenty years.

What others notice about the recluse is a metaphoric glass wall that seems to come up as soon as closer contact is attempted – you can look, but please don't touch. Conversations don't usually get far, and should any curious questions be asked, they are either ignored or cut short in some other way.

The recluse will have few visitors and those that call will either visit rarely or, if they call on a regular basis, will only ever appear on a particular day at a particular hour.

People on the outside tend to take little interest in the recluse because their efforts to make contact are not reciprocated or encouraged.

VIEW FROM THE INSIDE

The keyword here is 'routine'. Again, the regularity of activities and the fixed times when events take place provide a structure to the day; the adherence to the day's schedule assumes a meaning of its own. Interruptions from the outside world, such as neighbours wanting to chat, constitute a worry because they threaten to interrupt the regular course of procedure.

The recluse may have chosen his or her hermit existence out of a general disappointment with the world. When you feel that you cannot rely on others because your trust has been misused too often, you may decide to withdraw from the world and thereby shut out the possibility of any further frustration. It seems easier to forego potential pleasures than lay yourself open to being hurt again.

The characters in television programmes often become more real to the recluse than people in the outside world. At least on television, justice is always done; the good are rewarded and the bad punished, even if it takes sixty episodes.

In a similar way, a pet may take over as the focus of interest. You can fuss over it and speak to it and interpret all its responses as positive and appreciative of the care you bestow on it. You are making your pet happy, and that makes you happy. This is a simple, straightforward equation; no doubts, no complications, no need to worry that your pet will desert you. As it is totally dependent on you, you can be sure that it will remain loyal, and in this respect it is far better than a human companion.

However, recluses long for human company, but they cannot allow themselves to trust anyone enough to get involved, so the conflict ultimately remains unresolved.

EXPLANATIONS

The recluse has built up a self-protection mechanism that makes Fort Knox look as secure as a soaked-through shoe box. Once routines are firmly established they become a necessity, and any deviations cause anxiety and hurried attempts to re-establish the old pattern. Even if the recluse is forced to leave his or her familiar surroundings, they will endeavour to implement as much of their domestic routine as possible. Routine is felt to be reassuring and safe, a protective shield against the uncertainties of the outside world.

It is a brave man (or woman) who tries to become part of that routine and thus penetrate into the world of the recluse. Generally, a loner will guard his or her privacy rigorously, the underlying problem being that a recluse does not really see a need to let go of their old ways. It has taken them so long to establish their defence system, so why should they suddenly knock down that wall between themselves and the world?

If you feel that you come under the category of a recluse and you want to do something about it, the best way is to change your routine very slightly by cautiously and gradually letting other people back into your life. Choose carefully the people with whom you associate; that way you keep risks to a minimum.

If all else fails, it may be a good idea to work through your past experiences with a psychologist who will help you understand what went wrong and give you new confidence in yourself and your abilities.

THE PARTY-GOER

The party-goer is someone whose idea of fatal embarrassment is to be found at home on a Saturday evening.

VIEW FROM THE OUTSIDE

Here we have the exact opposite of the recluse. The party-goer is always on the move, always socializing, always having a good time. Wherever something is going on, the party-goer will appear. Dinner parties, cocktail parties, night clubs, discotheques, office functions, house-warmings – the party-goer will be there. Sometimes they will go from one event to another in the course of an evening so as not to miss out on anything. They seem to have an unlimited supply of energy, working during the day and socializing most nights. They laugh and joke a lot, they know an amazing number of people and they always seem to get invited wherever there is a social event.

The party-goer knows what is 'in' or 'out', has all the right clothes for all possible occasions and is rarely found at home in the evenings, and most certainly not at weekends. Party-goers are usually part of a clique of people whose main aim is to create opportunities to go out together. Often, these groups will also go on holiday together.

From the outside, the party-goer single seems to lead a carefree life. He or she always has something to look forward to, always enjoys life, and is always happy and easy-going. On the other hand, they seem to be smoking and drinking a bit too much and don't appear to have many (if any) close relationships. The party-goer seemingly epitomizes the advantages of singledom – an easy life and the freedom to do whatever they please whenever they please because there is no one else whose permission has to be sought. It's the life in the fast lane which looks glamorous when looked at from a terraced house in suburbia with a family and two children. The party-goer must surely be happy, being so popular and flitting from one party to the next?

VIEW FROM THE INSIDE

There are two different groups of people who come under the party-going category. The first comprises young people between the ages of 16 and 24 who suddenly discover that there is more to life than studying and working. The other group is made up of people who are between 25 and 55 and still have not found their feet.

Let's look at the younger group first. When you go to college or university you don't usually know anyone, so it is only natural that you should make friends with others in your project group or on your course. You enjoy their company because you have a lot in common. You share the same environment, the same interests, likes and dislikes, and all that pulls you together. The group is your 'home' and gives you a feeling of belonging, so you tend to do a lot of things together. Being in a situation away from the parental home and the rules and regulations of school, you begin to try out all those things that were previously restricted. You stay up late even though you have got to get up early and you extend your social life to breaking-point.

A similar situation arises when you start work at 17 or 18. You suddenly realize that you are on the verge of entering the responsibilities of adulthood, and before life gets too serious you want to enjoy yourself. When you are earning your own money for the first time, it feels wonderful to spend it on your own entertainment. The feeling of independence and freedom is exhilarating, and you intend to make the most of it while it lasts.

The other group of party-goers is that of older people who are in jobs but have not developed emotionally since their younger days. Seeing and being seen is no longer only a pleasure, it has become a necessity. When partying has been your main occupation besides working, you may have had little time left for other interests. This makes partying difficult to abandon because there is nothing with which to replace it.

Parties and clubbing provide excitement and an escape from the drabness of everyday life. You change into nice clothes, you are carried away by the dynamics of the crowd and the alcohol, you thrive on the hyped-up mood of the evening. Conversation is light, people know your name and easy confidences are exchanged. Everyone seems to be in a good mood, looking splendid and on top of the world. This mood is like an addiction as it blots out the reality of your life which might not look quite so rosy. Acquaintances made on these occasions tend to be superficial and party-goers prefer this as they are inclined to shun close relationships which would force them to reveal their real selves.

However, there comes a point when partying becomes tiring. Depending on your constitution, you can only get away with so much drink and so many sleepless nights; at some stage your body will refuse to co-operate. When this happens, you are really thrown back on your own resources. As your friendships are only shallow, there is little chance of anyone taking a particular interest in your disappearance from the scene, except as an excuse for gossip. If you have nothing except the partying in common with others, your highs can only last until the door has closed on the last guest. Inside you are always aware that you need something more substantial to fill the internal void, but then you can just about make it to the next party, so you decide not to worry just yet.

EXPLANATIONS

It obviously makes a difference whether you are a party-goer as part of a certain phase in your life or whether it is a mode of living per se.

It is certainly a valuable experience at some point to spend time dancing the night away with a group of people you like, and there is nothing wrong with doing this excessively for a while. It can be a worthwhile experience that teaches you your own limitations and allows you to try out a certain way of living. What usually happens is that people experiment with partying and excessive drinking or drug-taking for a while and then, through choice or circumstances, move on to other things. However, being on a constant high can become boring when you no longer have a way of offsetting the highs against the lows, so the highs have to become better all the time so you can still recognize them as highs.

As long as you can perceive the artificiality of constant partying, you will find it easy to establish a balance that allows room for more meaningful relationships and pursuits. If, however, you have a lot of personal problems that you feel unable to solve, it is easier to ignore them by being in a jolly environment as often as possible. As a rule of thumb you can say that whatever you do to excess is a sign that you are running away from something else.

Unfortunately, running away doesn't solve the basic problems. Many of those compulsive party-goers are slaves to their habit. Latent depression and nervous tension drive them increasingly to escape their inner reality. They need to be acknowledged as being desirable because they lack a sense of self-esteem. As they are not sure of themselves, it is of great importance that they should be invited to as many social events as possible.

They continually need other people's approval to bolster their brittle egos. Even though they may find that in the company of others their self-doubts are temporarily lifted, their positive moods last only briefly.

THE CAREER PERSON

The career person is someone who, for the last 20 years, has been determined to think about a holiday or a relationship as soon as they have a moment to spare.

VIEW FROM THE OUTSIDE

Immaculately groomed at all times, the career person looks like something out of an advertisement in a glossy magazine. No matter how late the conference, no matter how exhausting their schedule on the previous day, the next morning they are awake and in control and ready to tackle the next lot of decisions. Everyone can see that they mean business, and their business is to climb the career ladder. They have set themselves a target and they go for it one hundred per cent. They take work home and go into the office at the weekend; if necessary, they sacrifice their evenings for an important project and they generally seem to be attached by an invisible umbilical cord to their computer at the office.

Career people are punctual, tidy and competent. They deal with emergencies at work efficiently and quickly; they know what they are doing. They don't seem to have a private life; how else could they get through their mountains of work? They obviously don't have anyone at home who gives them a hard time for doing all this overtime.

The career person is determined to accomplish every task to a high standard, and they expect the same dedication and commitment from the people who work with them. When they don't find the co-operation they want, career people can easily become irritable or unpleasant because they feel that they are being held back by other people's inadequacies. In order to avoid these delays they prefer to do things themselves rather than delegate; that way they know that the results are going to be satisfactory, even though it means a longer working day for them.

Conversations with the career person are usually restricted to issues concerned with work or current political affairs.

In one way or another, the career person manages to stay aloof from colleagues. It is as if personal contacts would hamper his or her impetus to get on with their career development.

VIEW FROM THE INSIDE

Being perfect has its price. In order to be turned out well every day and still cope with a tiring workload, you need to invest a lot of energy and willpower. As you set yourself high standards, you have to work hard to achieve them.

Initially, it is gratifying to have reached your first target and know that you have performed exceptionally well, but now the struggle begins. The next project needs to be equally successful, if not more so, or you will feel you have failed, even though you may still be way above average.

Career people feel driven by a need to achieve and a need to be best. Promotion to them is nothing but the official recognition that indeed they *are* the best, and this is of utmost importance. All their energies are invested in their ambition, and therefore their private life has to take second place. Intrusions such as family matters are seen as a nuisance that distract from the only real issue in the career person's life – work. When they get home from work, there is no time left to do anything except have a quick meal and then go to bed to recharge the batteries for the next day. Social activities are largely avoided because the career person is too tired after work. As a consequence, any friendships they may have don't

get enough attention and often wither away so that in
the end, there is hardly any social life left. This, in turn,
makes it even easier for them to focus on their work
because there is virtually nothing else to which they need
to direct their attention.

Making a relationship work may look a lot less gratifying because it is not an official achievement, whereas
being in a good professional position with lots of money
and externally visible perks like a company car are
accomplishments that are noticed by the outside world.
This gives the career person that feeling of self-worth
they want.

EXPLANATIONS

The key to the career person's way of life lies in his or
her need for public recognition. It is as if they have to
prove themselves again and again in order to receive
official praise and tangible proof of their achievements
by way of a better job title or a higher salary.

Even though career people appear so competent and
in control, their zeal is born out of a feeling of inadequacy
and worthlessness. There is invariably a childhood his-
tory of non-acknowledgement of emotional needs where
the only thing that counted was academic performance,
or an upbringing where needs were ignored or suppressed. However, those needs for love, attention and
security are fundamental, and when they are repressed,
rather than disappear, they become a problem in some
other way, albeit on a subconscious level.

It is from this subconscious level that the drive arises
to gain other people's acceptance. When there has been
a lack of recognition in childhood, people can spend the
rest of their lives trying to achieve it. Recognition is one
of the prerequisites for feeling good and liking yourself.
As it is difficult to live without some sort of self-esteem,
the career person has to make up for their negative feelings about themselves by becoming particularly good at
something in life, and very often that is work.

By concentrating on their careers, they are also avoiding

the perilous area of human contact which has already proved to be unsatisfactory. In this way, the career person kills two birds with one stone – they avoid the deep waters of interpersonal relationships and therefore can dedicate all their efforts to the pursuit of self-esteem via their job.

This way of life lacks balance and true satisfaction. The career person can forge a satisfactory professional image after a while, but not an equally valid personal image. Apart from the fact that you cannot work hard all the time, the time will come when you are too old to work, and then there is nothing left. Having put all your eggs in one basket, you have never had the time to build up a private life, and to try to do so once you have retired is quite difficult.

THE BEGINNER SOLOIST

This is someone who asks for a table behind a pillar in a restaurant and then tries to blend in with the wallpaper.

VIEW FROM THE OUTSIDE

You can spot the beginner soloist quite easily when you are staying in an hotel. As you are sitting in the dining room, you observe a young man coming in, with his eyes firmly fixed to the ground. When the waiter addresses him it nearly makes him jump. You feel terribly sorry and embarrassed for him, hoping that, in a moment, his parents will come down, but they don't. Now you know that you are looking at a novice at the game, someone who has an invisible learner plate on his back.

In the supermarket, the beginner soloist is found wandering between the rows of shelves with a little wire basket containing just one packet of Oxo-cubes. They are not terribly sure what they need or what they want and seem somewhat overawed by the variety of goods that are available. Once they have reached the cash desk, they still only have the Oxo-cubes and a cauliflower cheese meal for one in their basket. You can see that they realize this is not enough, but they don't know what else to get.

Beginner soloists tend to smile a lot and apologize all the time. Conversations with them are somewhat unsatisfactory because they tend to agree with whatever you say and don't really seem to have an opinion of their own. They don't have a lot of practical experience and are easily impressed by other people's achievements, be they real or imagined. They are not sure about anything and are eternally grateful to you if you save them from having to make their own decisions.

This category of singles consists either of very young and inexperienced people or of very shy ones who lack self-confidence. In most cases, however, this is only a temporary phase they are going through. As the very young become older, they gain in experience and as the shy ones achieve some successes they feel more self-confident and, at least on the outside, seem to cope better.

VIEW FROM THE INSIDE

Beginner soloists struggle with feelings of insecurity and fear; they feel under permanent scrutiny from the outside world and are convinced that they will be found lacking. Low self-esteem and lack of expertise in practical matters make them feel inadequate and hopeless, and this can in some cases lead to a state of panic when they have to deal with unknown situations. They feel very much alone in their fight against the difficulties of life and have a tendency to overlook the fact that half their problems would be solved if they were to persist in their efforts of gathering more experience.

Most beginners soon get the hang of organizing their lives satisfactorily, at least on the practical level, and that gives them a feeling of success and therefore confidence. If, however, it so happens that several of their first adventures as singles go wrong, they may understandably feel defeated and give up and ultimately even withdraw (see the recluse). With every failure they become more convinced that they cannot cope and that this is because they are failures as human beings. Ultimately, this can become a self-fulfilling prophecy that makes them fail simply because they *expect* to fail.

At best, the beginner soloist feels that life is beyond their control. They find themselves in a new mode of life where they are not sure of the rules. They have left the relative safety of their family or their relationship and now they are without a structure to which they can cling. For many people, this does not constitute a problem because they have had the opportunity to establish self-esteem and practical skills in their previous relationships with their families or their partners. If this has not happened, however, the person often feels helpless and abandoned once they are on their own.

EXPLANATIONS

'New' singles are like any other beginners. Whether you have just bought your first car, your first dog or your first pair of roller skates, you are bound to make a number of mistakes until you get it right. Nobody expects to be able to manage perfectly when it comes to acquiring such skills, and this is why there are courses on offer and evening classes and lessons. And yet, leaving home or leaving a relationship seems to be a sink-or-swim situation for most, with no official help on offer.

Much depends on how well prepared you are. As with everything else, it certainly helps if you have an outgoing personality and good communication skills. You cannot change your basic personality, but even if you are the quiet type, you can learn to overcome your shyness (more about this in Chapter 6). Communication skills, on the other hand, are something you would normally learn at home, but if your parents have had problems expressing themselves you may not have had a good start in this respect. Again, this is something you can

learn later. The only thing you need is the willingness
to acquire new skills.

In this respect, the beginner soloist has every chance
of succeeding. Initial problems need not grow from mole-
hills into mountains! Provided you don't give up and
you persist in getting what you want, those first stumbling blocks need only be a passing phase. With practice
you will become better and more successful and, as a
consequence, more sure of yourself.

The necessary skills are discussed in the following
chapter. Try out a few new ways of 'being', it is all part
and parcel of growing up. Being able to stand on your
own two feet is a useful skill to have, not just for the
time you spend on your own, but also later on should
you decide to get involved in a relationship. In both
cases you need to know what you want and how to get
it.

THE WOULD-BE SINGLE

The would-be single is someone who is marginally more
terrorized by the thought of being single than by the
thought of staying with their partner.

VIEW FROM THE OUTSIDE

The would-be single spends a lot of time talking about
the advantages of being on their own, but somehow they
never follow it up. Usually, those long speeches about
bachelorhood are sparked off by an unsatisfactory domestic situation where the partnership does not work out.
It is amazing, though, how bad a relationship can
become without the injured party ever making that step
and moving out. When everyone around them starts
getting exasperated with the situation, the would-be
single appears to be quite happy to complain about their
relationship to anyone who will listen. The only thing
they are obviously unwilling to do is to put their words
into practice.

They may make attempts to move out, and some of them will even get their friends involved in helping them, but in the end they invariably change their minds. Either it is not the right time, or they feel they want to give the relationship yet another chance, or they openly admit that they lack the courage actually to move out. One of my clients got her sister to make all the necessary arrangements for her and find her a flat, but when the moment came to leave, she was unable to confront her boyfriend with the facts, and stayed.

Once the would-be single has cried wolf a few times, relatives and friends give up on them and often withdraw because they begin to think that the relationship cannot be that bad if the would-be single is not prepared to make more serious efforts to move out.

VIEW FROM THE INSIDE

When you are in a relationship that doesn't work out, being on your own appears to be the ideal solution. Remove the object of aggravation, namely the present partner, and hey presto, you are happy! Would-be singles have a great yearning for the advantages of going solo, but at the same time an even greater fear of how they will cope on their own.

It has usually been a long time since they have been on their own; some of them may never have lived by themselves. Maybe there was a time before they were married when they led their own life; maybe they went straight from their parents' home to the marital home and therefore were never able to test their own strengths. The less practice you have in being independent, the less you feel you can trust your own abilities and resourcefulness. Therefore, being a single looks like the promised land, but the path to it appears very rocky indeed.

All those things your partner provides for you at the moment you will have to take care of yourself should you decide to leave. From companionship and entertainment to doing the laundry and filling in the tax forms, it is all going to be in your hands. It is like being employed to do one job and then being forced to take on an additional one for which you don't feel qualified.

Many people shy away from the prospect of having to learn new skills. All they see is an apparent mass of new conditions and circumstances if they decided to cut the, albeit damaged, ties with their partner, and that is enough to scare them into staying in the relationship. Present conditions may be unacceptable, but at least they provide safety, even if it is safety in unhappiness. To make a break from that relationship would mean to leave well-known territory and venture into new areas, and who knows what you might let yourself in for should you do so? It is the fear of the unknown, coupled with an inability to assess your own strength that often bars the way into an ultimately happier future.

EXPLANATIONS

Change can appear threatening at the best of times, and the would-be single certainly feels ill at ease at the prospect of confronting the unknown. Rationally, they can see the advantages of leaving their present situation, but emotionally, something is holding them back. It is this inner conflict that makes most would-be singles go for a compromise situation – they wait until someone else comes along who can take over the function of 'new partner'. That way they don't have to face any drastic changes such as going through a split-up, while at the same time having to find their own place or providing their own entertainment. They simply allow themselves to be transferred from one relationship into another, hoping that the new partner will miraculously produce all those qualities which their previous partner lacked.

Initially, it all seems to work out. Their innermost wishes appear to come true – until the honeymoon period is over and the new partner turns out to have faults, just like the previous one, and they are back to square one.

Often, it is the inability to be alone that prevents people from trying out the option of being single. This is often due to a general lack of self-confidence instilled in childhood where the child is not allowed to express his or her own wishes and therefore ignores them. This leads to the feeling that you should not have any needs, but of course your needs are still there. Moodiness or depression are sure signals that your needs are not met adequately in your present environment, but you feel unable to express this. Instead, you sulk or withdraw. You are boiling inside with anger, but at the same time you feel incompetent and totally unable to be without the person who is causing you all these problems. Consequently moving out is not an option for you.

Fear of loneliness is possibly the greatest stumbling block for a would-be single. However, being able to stand on your own two feet emotionally and socially is part of being an adult; the inability to do so is a sign of immaturity. It is essential that you learn to understand about your own needs and learn about your own strengths in order to live life to the full, be it in a relationship or on your own.

If you are unhappy with your partner, you need to have options at your disposal that do not include another partner, otherwise you are not choosing that new partner freely. When the new man or woman in your life is only a stop-gap or an escape from loneliness, nobody wins.

THE FANATIC SOLOIST

This is someone who runs a mile when they hear the word 'relationship' and a marathon when they hear the word 'marriage'.

VIEW FROM THE OUTSIDE

Here we have the King and Queen of the One-Night-Stand. They are charming, witty and entertaining; they say all the right things at the right time to whoever they are going out with that evening. They are ideal companions. They listen attentively to what their partner is saying, they flatter in the nicest possible way and make you feel that you are very special to them; in other words, they seem to be the ideal partner – until you have been to bed with them. Suddenly, relations begin to cool off, the charm disappears and what is left is a man or a woman who only dreads one thing – commitment. They are single and they have every intention of staying single, and anyone who tries to invade their territory is in for an unpleasant surprise.

Similar to the party-goer, the fanatic single is usually the dynamic type, often professionally very successful and well-organized in their private life. They are attractive because they seem to have their life under control and they make decisions easily and effortlessly. They seem to have no problems. The outside world sees the fanatic single as interested in others because they are helpful and considerate when someone is in trouble. They give sound advice and are willing to sort things out for you when you get stuck.

They are lovely people, as long as they set the terms. The picture changes dramatically as soon as someone tries to become part of their life. This is when the fanatic single can become ice-cold and even cruel. Charm and smooth-talking will disappear should you fail to understand that they are not at your beck and call and are certainly in no way prepared to tie themselves down to one person. They want to play the field and make their own rules, and no one is allowed into their private life unless invited, and so far, no invitations have been issued.

Fanatic singles exude an aura of strict control. They lay down the law; they control themselves and their environment, their household, their professional life and their pastimes. When you get to know them a bit better, having observed their actions and behaviour for a while, it becomes apparent how desperately important it is for them to stick rigidly to their self-imposed rules. There is no room for deviations, there are no shades between black and white. They declare that they are single and that they want to be single because relationships are nothing but trouble and don't last anyway. They were not made to be tied down by marriage, provide for a wife or look after a husband; they prefer to stay on the surface of relationships and go through the exciting first stages only, but otherwise preserve their freedom.

VIEW FROM THE INSIDE

All is well for the fanatic as long as the world plays by their rules. The rules serve as a protective structure and support system that was erected originally to shield them from getting hurt. In fact, everything in the fanatic's life is geared towards protection and safety of their own person. Their charm, attentiveness, and even their helpfulness ensure that other people like them, and it is a hurtful blow to their ego if they cannot extract daily demonstrations of admiration or gratitude from their fellow human beings, in particular from the opposite sex.

The fanatic soloist needs other people, not because he or she wants to love, but because he or she loves to be wanted, and they will unscrupulously manipulate others to achieve that aim. Once they get someone to admire them, they lose interest because they have no intention of dealing with the consequences. Although they are dependent on other people's adoration, once someone begins to depend on them, they despise them and off they go to conquer the next victim. Manipulation is the name of the game, and the fanatic soloist is expert at it.

This does not mean, however, that fanatics are necessarily happy on their own, but it is the only way in which they can live since they cannot cope with relationships and true intimacy. Rather than feeling inadequate they elect to be solo and, consequently, make it into a virtue. If no one gets close, no one can find out about how brittle their ego really is and how little they have to give.

EXPLANATIONS

As a rule of thumb you can say that the more rigid someone is in their outlook, the more frightened they are, and that also applies to our fanatic soloist. Looking at him or her from the outside, this may sound incredible because they appear so self-assured and in control. But control is only necessary when there is a feeling of underlying chaos, and this is very much the case with the fanatic.

In many cases, the fanatic comes from a background where love from the parent of the opposite sex was not forthcoming, for whatever reason. A father who despises women will reject his daughters; a mother who mistrusts men will not accept her son. This is a terrible predicament for a child to be in. On the one hand you need that love for your emotional well-being, on the other hand you hate the parent for not giving this love to you. It is very much this love-hate feeling that will later on determine your relationships with others.

You now have two options as a child. You can either try to win the parent's affection by pleasing them and, for example, work extra hard at school; or you can withdraw and tell yourself that it doesn't matter. In the first case, there is the possibility that you will become a workaholic later in life, still trying to prove to your mother or father that you are worth loving (see also the career person). In the second instance, you might give up on relationships and remove yourself from society altogether (see the recluse) or alternatively maintain only a superficial contact with others which is what the fanatic does. The hurt during childhood years has been so great that it must not be allowed to happen ever again, so you build up those barricades of control which make it impossible for others to get close to you. You have hardened yourself against any feelings of compassion, empathy or love, and if you detect them in others you consider them a weakness. Childhood has taught you that love does not exist, so you get on with life and tidy away any messy feelings by suppressing them.

The motto of the fanatic soloist is 'Don't get involved

or you'll get hurt', and as long as you stick to it, you may be lonely but you will be safe. Should anyone try to cross the line by getting involved with you, then this is their problem. They show their weakness by being dependent on affection and intimacy, and they therefore deserve no better than to be thrown out. After all, it never did you any harm to be unloved as a child!

THE DESPERATE SINGLE

The desperate single is someone who doesn't like to be single, has never wanted to be single and doesn't want to stay single and therefore behaves like the back end of a pantomime horse that has lost its front half.

VIEW FROM THE OUTSIDE

How do you spot the desperate single? Imagine a party or an office function or any other form of informal social gathering. The desperate single is the person who talks a lot at (not to) someone of the opposite sex and has them practically nailed to the wall as they do so. The female desperado may also be standing too close to her victim, at a point where the lack of physical distance is just on the verge of being uncomfortable for her partner. You can see him trying to edge away, sideways or backwards, but she inevitably manages to corner him somehow. She is over-enthusiastic and exudes a sense of pressure. The untrained eye will attribute this urgency to the topic on which she is delivering a monologue, but the expert singles-spotter knows that the real reason for this undercurrent of urgency is the imperative need to find a partner.

The male desperado, on the other hand, can often be found wandering around the female party population, searching for someone to give him attention and show interest in him or in what he is saying. With the tiniest bit of encouragement, he will fasten himself to a lady like a pilot fish to a whale. After the merest fifteen minutes of conversation, he will ask her out, and if she turns him down, he just goes back on his round, looking for another candidate. It almost seems that it does not matter *who* agrees to go out with him, as long as *somebody* does. Of course, as soon as the other women realize what he is doing, his chances of actually getting a date that evening are considerably diminished because no one wants to be the second choice.

This is more or less the general effect the desperate single has on others. People are often put off by the single's fervent attempts or just find them a bit ridiculous. The more the desperados try, the further they remove themselves from their goal. There is nothing like desperate urgency to deter a potential partner.

VIEW FROM THE INSIDE

The curious thing about desperate singles is that they are not really interested in the people they pursue, even though it appears so from the outside. The driving force behind their endeavours is a feeling of need, an overpowering sense of having to overcome their single status, and therefore anyone who shows willing and seems reasonably acceptable will do. There is a tendency to look at the potential future partner in an unrealistic way, *wanting* him or her to be the right one, *wanting* it all to work out. The rose-tinted spectacles make the potential relationship take on larger-than-life proportions. The first chat at the party is enough to trigger off feverish thoughts of moving in together, the first date already has wedding bells ringing in the desperado's mind.

The ultimate four-letter word for the desperate single is 'wait'. They are not prepared to get to know the other person or assess their background and personality slowly over a period of time. Compatibility is not considered an issue since the single person, at that stage, is ready to do anything to make that relationship work, change themselves and mould themselves to the requirements of the partner, just as long as they have someone by their side to prove to the world that they have not been left on the shelf. Their inability to be by themselves pushes them forward leaving pride and prudence behind.

In this way, warning signals are often overlooked. When it is patently clear to everyone around them that their prospective new partner is unsuitable, the desperate single has blinkers on that prevent them from seeing reality. They don't want to know if anything is wrong, and even if they are aware of their partner's shortcomings, they feel a compulsion to go through with their venture anyway for fear of losing the one person who has shown interest in them.

The longer this situation goes on, the more likely it is that the single will lower his or her standards. Generally, their standards have never been very high in the first place, otherwise they would not feel this urgent need to procure a partner for themselves, and certainly not in this self-effacing manner.

EXPLANATIONS

Just as desperate singles lack self-confidence, they also lack critical insight into others, and each problem makes the other worse. It is a vicious circle whereby you have little self-esteem and therefore assess other people as worthier than yourself, and as a consequence, you are unable to perceive their faults.

Lack of self-esteem and uncritical adoration of others puts you in a vulnerable position when you are unhappy as a single and you are less likely to pick a suitable partner. It will also make your life more difficult, because in your opinion your single status adds to your worthlessness.

When you are unsure of yourself and don't really like yourself, any sense of worthiness has to come from outside. This basic insecurity means that there is nothing to keep your self-respect going when you are on your own. Success in your job will make life easier, but this is not considered essential.

People who lack self-confidence will often attribute their professional achievements to luck or coincidence, even though they have clearly worked very hard to get where they are. They are often plagued by fears of 'being found out', their nightmare being that one day, the boss will walk in and tell them to their face that they are just *pretending* to be competent. They feel like a cheat for having reached their professional rank and feel they have to work extra hard to make up for their deceit.

As they cannot supply themselves with moral support or appreciation, but at the same time feel empty and desolate without it, they need to get recognition from a partner. The partner's function is to provide the official message to the world that the desperate single is lovable and special and therefore worth living with or, ideally, marrying. In other words, the potential partner is the crutch that supports the single's faltering self-esteem. The relationship has very little to do with love.

But how can a person's self-confidence be so low that they get themselves into this position in the first place? There are various explanations for this, but two of the main components are certainly personality and upbringing. When you grow up in an environment where you are not appreciated as a worthwhile person who deserves attention, it can make it harder for you to achieve self-respect. If this is coupled with a shy and retiring personality, the problem is exacerbated further.

It is, however, always possible to work on your lack of confidence. Sometimes we learn to trust ourselves through experiences whereby we begin to recognize our own strengths; sometimes we come across the right person at the right time (and this does *not* have to be a partner!) from whom we can learn confidence. If all else fails, we can always seek professional help. It is our privilege to decide whether we want to stay unhappy or change our life for the better.

6. . . . And How to Avoid Them!

So now you know about all the things that can go wrong and all the things you are afraid *might* go wrong when you are single. In the last two chapters, we have been concerned with what most people are worried about when they think of spending a prolonged period of time without a partner.

The reason why I think it is important to discuss these worries is because we tend to feel inadequate when something troubles us. We think that it is our own incompetence that prevents us from moving effortlessly into a new phase of life. However, a certain amount of unease is normal when changes occur in your life. What is unnecessary is to let this period of worrying and self-doubt drag on indefinitely.

When you have just lost your partner, you feel as if your single status stretches in front of you for eternity, as if there is never going to be another man/woman for you. Of course, none of us ever knows how long we will be single, whether it will be five weeks, five months or five years. But equally, none of us can ever know the good things that are just round the corner. Even the most hardened soloist is not immune to a new partner walking into their life and turning it upside down. So why not have a good time while waiting for just that to happen? Or why not have a good time, full stop? In the following chapters, you will find detailed discussions about various ways of achieving just that.

There are lots of things you can do to help yourself. By working on your self-confidence, your social skills and your personal growth, you will ensure not only a happier time for yourself, but you will also develop into a more interesting person.

COPING WITH CHANGE

To many people, there is something really frightening about change. Starting a new job, moving house, becoming a father, the death of a close friend, or even everyday events like going on holiday, all imply change in one way or another. Any new idea or situation necessitates altering old patterns, but even if the old ways were inconvenient and bothersome, they were at least familiar. You may not feel very stimulated by your little flat in the middle of Birmingham, but at least you know you can brew a decent cup of tea in your kitchen. You are not so sure whether the same can be said of your holiday resort in Ibiza! Similarly, you may feel very happy about your promotion, but at the same time you are doubtful about your ability to cope with your new responsibilities. Maybe you have been too bold in your attempt to climb the career ladder?

Of course, the same is true when you are faced with being single when you have been used to having someone else around. You feel out of your depth, unsure of yourself and, above all, you lack a structure to hang on to. A job can be very helpful in providing a framework on a professional level. It can give you security while you are getting used to your new status. Sometimes, a job can even take care of some of your social needs if you get on well with your colleagues, but this is not always the case. Often you are still left with the responsibility to re-organize your social life yourself.

The knack of coping with change lies in controlling your thinking because the main threat comes from over-thinking. Let me give you an example. Let us assume you have been separated from your partner for a while and are spending another night on your own. Your bed is nice and warm but somehow empty without the other person, and you cannot sleep. It is dark outside, there is nothing on television, and you lie there with your eyes open and you start thinking. The way it usually goes is like this: 'No more snoring, thank God for that . . . How come I miss the snoring then? . . . Oh, I really don't know what I want. Maybe this is all a big mistake . . . My God, what have I done? Maybe I should have stuck it out a bit longer, maybe it would have worked out after all. Now I'm here, all on my own, and there are thousands of nights like this ahead of me . . . What is wrong with me? Why can't I keep a relationship? Maybe my standards are simply too high? . . . I'll never find anyone again, I'm just incapable of seeing a relationship through. I'm just not attractive/intelligent/well-read/interesting enough.' Etcetera, etcetera. This monologue could go on until the early hours of the morning if your body wasn't intelligent enough to send you to sleep at some point. However, by that stage the damage is already done. Your confidence is rock-bottom and the future looks desperately black.

The strange thing about nights is that they make things look different, negative and hopeless. The reason for this is that, as you are getting tired, your logical mind, the ever watchful guard dog in front of the gates to your subconscious, is beginning to doze off a little, and all the fears and doubts you have accumulated over the last few months start creeping out. Have you noticed how the next morning life doesn't look quite so bleak? This is because now your logical mind stands to attention again and tells you that surely there must be someone out there who is compatible with you, that all is not lost, and anyway, you don't really look so bad after all . . . If, however, you have lost this feeling of optimism altogether, it means that your past still has a very firm grip on you and will not allow you to move forward with confidence. If this is the case, you will have to deal with the past first before you can get on with your future. As one interviewee said:

'No matter how hard I tried to forget her, she was always on my mind. I knew it wasn't doing me any good to dwell on the past, but I just couldn't help it – in the end I went to see a counsellor, and he helped me sort it all out.'

KEEP A DIARY

Keeping a diary is an effective way of getting your thoughts sorted out. The problem with thoughts is that they have a tendency to run riot unless we can externalize them in one way or another. As long as we do not speak about them or write them down, we cannot measure them against reality, and this is when they can get out of proportion. Writing down what we find ourselves thinking about forces us to embark on an assessment process whereby we have to sift and work through what has happened in the past. This can help us to come to terms with the past more easily and opens the way to adapting to new situations.

If you find it difficult to start writing, consider for a moment what exactly it is that has changed. Include everything, your general circumstances, friendships that have ended because your partner is no longer around, difficulties you encounter because you are on your own, and all the various and possibly contradictory feelings you discover in yourself. You may be surprised that you can harbour two entirely opposing emotions at the same time. Widowed people are often upset to find that besides missing their partner, they are also angry at them. This doesn't seem to make sense because you are not supposed to think ill of someone you love, and yet, this is the feeling they have! They feel angry at having been left behind to cope with life on their own, and then they feel guilty and ashamed at their inner tirade at someone who can't defend themself any more.

If you do not confront these feelings, they get tangled up and produce chaos. By writing them down you create a certain order in your mind. This does not mean that all your troubles are over, but it helps you take the edge off the painful process of letting go. As you work through your feelings and memories, they gradually begin to change, as if you had turned a colour photograph into a black and white one. There is no point in pretending that the past has never happened. Old memories will come into your mind, whether you want them to or not, so you might as well use them to your advantage. You cannot launch yourself into the future if the past still ties you down. Put your thoughts down on paper, and eventually you will be able to file them away where they can't do any damage to you any longer. When you take a thought out of your head and look at it, it changes, and when you put it back into your head it is never the same.

TALKING ABOUT THE CHANGE

Ideally you know someone who has been through your situation and understands how you feel. Talking to someone else is similar to writing it down in that it enables you to externalize your feelings in a constructive way. Moreover, it has the advantage of allowing you a reaction from someone else as you voice your thoughts. Even if the other person does not really understand your situation, it can be reassuring to feel that someone is on your side. Sympathy gives you some warmth and strength to help you carry on.

It can prove to be constructive to hear what someone else makes of those past events, and your friend might be able to add some of their own observations. Sometimes we feel petty and narrow-minded about having been upset about our ex-partner's idiosyncrasies, only to find that a friend found them just as annoying. Suddenly our guilt evaporates; what a relief! So we were right to be annoyed after all. We know our friend to be a sensible person, so if they feel the same way we do then it means we are not just over-reacting.

For most people, this private moral support is sufficient to carry them through the most difficult patches, but sometimes it may not be enough and professional help has to be sought.

Inability to let go of a past relationship can ruin your life. Walking around like a zombie because you cannot stop thinking about your ex-partner can cost you your health and also your job. In my practice I see quite a few clients who are self-employed or in a very high position with a lot of responsibility who are faced with just that problem. They know that unless they get the past relationship trauma sorted out they will go bankrupt or get into serious difficulties at work, simply because they cannot concentrate any more or make rational decisions. Working through the past helps them put events into perspective. This not only makes their situation less painful but also lessens their feelings of despair. They begin to adopt a new attitude and see themselves in a more positive light again.

With the help of hypnosis, analysis can be quick and efficient, and often these results are achieved in less than eight sessions. (For case studies, see *Positive Thinking* and *Strategies of Optimism*.)

IF YOU CAN'T BEAT 'EM, JOIN 'EM

Sometimes it makes sense to do an absurd thing. If you don't like the changes that were forced upon you, create some more changes of your own. If your girlfriend has left you, redecorate her room in your favourite wallpaper. If your husband has died, change the furniture in the house, rearrange the living room, make the study into a bedroom or the dining room into a second reception room. If you have to endure unpleasant change, you might as well get something out of it by adding some alterations that are to your liking. As your life is already in turmoil, why not use the momentum and introduce some new ideas? You have nothing to lose.

It is in times of crisis that people take steps they would have considered too daring before, or too risky, or too unsettling. But once they are unsettled, they feel they have nothing to lose and that they might as well go the whole way. A friend of mine explained it like this:

'When Peter told me he was seeing someone else, I was so shocked I couldn't think straight for a few months. First I got angry at him, then I got lonely and then I got desperate.

And then I started thinking that I was getting fed up with being desperate, and I decided to do this training course in reflexology. I didn't care that I had to do it in my spare time – there was nothing else to do anyway. And this step has changed my life. With Peter around I would never have had the impetus to do it.'

A personal catastrophe in our lives can often bring out our true strengths, much to our own and everyone else's surprise.

The strange thing about change is that unless it is absolutely necessary, we resist it in any way we can. Change makes us nervous and we wish it would some-how go away so that we don't have to deal with it. The problem of course is that we have a preconception that change is negative, and this preconception tinges our subsequent behaviour. In order to overcome our negative concept of change we have to learn to separate our obser-vations from our preconceptions.

Most people see what they expect to see. When they find themselves on their own, without a partner, they expect to be unhappy because with their partner they were happy. And because they expect to be unhappy, they are unhappy. Women whose husbands used to do everything for them expect to be helpless on their own, so they are. What you expect will ultimately happen because you behave according to your expectations. If you believe that you cannot work the electric drill, you won't even try, and this means that you will indeed fail to learn to use it. If you expect to be incapable of operat-ing the washing machine, you will be reluctant to try. Only when you insist on tackling a new task will you give yourself a chance of progressing and taking control of your own life. And this brings me to my last point.

PRACTISE GETTING BETTER

So let us assume you have just got yourself into a situation where, through childhood experiences and teachings, you find yourself drifting into the I-will-never-be-able-to-get-used-to-this-change mode. Once you have been in this mode for a while, it becomes something of a habit. You will actually find that you are very talented at repeatedly thinking that you can't deal with your new life. In fact, you are perfect at it. (You can tell that you are perfect at it because you feel utterly miserable. If you hadn't convinced yourself so well, you would only be *slightly* miserable!) Now let's start practising something new because from my experience, people prefer to be happy rather than depressed. And don't worry – if you miss that gloomy feeling you can always go back to it. All you need to do is think in the old way.

However, just for a moment, let's assume you have a switch in your head that changes the polarity of your mind from negative to positive. Imagine for a moment what it would be like if you suddenly saw only the good aspects of your new situation. What is it that looks promising and encouraging? Nothing? OK, look again, very closely now. You will have to admit, sulkily and reluctantly, that there are one or two good points you can make out, and once you start looking for them, you will find more and more. Now dwell on these positive aspects for at least five minutes! (You never knew how long five minutes were; am I right?) Now check how you feel. Probably only a *little* bit better, but it is a start. Did you know that this is precisely the same way in which you became good at being unhappy? You started thinking about two or three negative sides of your situation and then worked your repertoire up to a dozen until you were *really* depressed. And this works the same way if you want to become happy. Practise thinking of as many optimistic thoughts as you can and prolong the time you spend thinking them and, hey presto, you have introduced a smile on to your face again. Feel the corners of your mouth turning upwards, and now, quick, look in the mirror. Looks good, doesn't it?

Now all the negative thoughts come flooding back; of course they do because they have been there for such a long time that they won't give up their position without a fight. Now your motto can be again 'If you can't beat 'em, join 'em.' Since the pessimistic thoughts are there now anyway, let's pursue them properly. This is how you do it. Think about yourself on your own, abandoned by the one you loved. You are feeling miserable and lonely and completely dejected. See yourself slouching in front of the television, feet on the coffee table, digging into an extra large family size packet of crisps, stuffing your face because you don't care how fat you are, you don't care at all, your eyes hypnotically glued to the screen, watching programmes you always hated because nothing matters anyway and then you slop down some more Fosters/Cinzano/Baileys Irish Cream, and then the doorbell goes and you go to answer it, crushing crisps into the carpet with your smelly socks, and as you open the door you see it is a colleague from work but you don't care; before you can say good evening to him you let out an enormous belch but it doesn't matter because you don't care anyway and the colleague is really embarrassed and leaves after a short while because you don't feel like talking so you just ignore him as he sits in the only armchair that's not littered with crumbs and empty beer cans and your last unsuccessful attempt at the *Evening Standard* crossword puzzle. This colleague then goes away and tells everyone else what a slob you've become, so you lose all your friends, and as you sit in front of your telly, you get fatter and fatter and in the end you die choking on a salt-and-vinegar crisp.

Check your face in the mirror again. The chances are you will be smiling again! You can do this with any negative thought. Take the scenario and spin it out into absurdity, and it loses its horror. Not only do you face your fears, but you also make them into something funny, and that gives you the upper hand.

DEVELOPING A POSITIVE SELF-IMAGE

Quite a few of those interviewed were aware of a considerable discrepancy between how they thought others saw them and the way they perceived themselves. Even though, on the outside, they might appear confident and successful, on the inside, they felt quite different and not half as glamorous.

We all seem to have this ability to live on two levels.

On the surface level, we display our skills and talents to the outside world. This is the showman level where we operate smoothly and effortlessly and where we keep our feelings strictly under control. It is when we are at work or socializing that the surface level is deployed; we are in a good mood and we are competent and self-confident.

However, when we are with family and friends or when we are alone, we tend to permit the other level to come to the fore; let's call it the intimate level. On this level, our feelings are much more prominent, especially those of self-doubt and insecurity. Because we are much more vulnerable when we show this side of ourselves, we tend to be very careful about whom we allow to see us like that. Some people cannot allow anyone to see them at this level at all, for example the recluse or the fanatic soloist. Some people cannot even allow themselves to look at this deeper level for fear of what they might find there. This can be a serious problem because no matter how effectively you think you control those unwanted feelings, they will always leak out here or there. By denying their existence, you can't make them go away. On the contrary, you give them much greater significance than they really have and you waste all your valuable energy on suppressing them, rather than dealing with them constructively.

People who only display their intimate level to the outside world, on the other hand, often do so to manipulate a situation. Telling others about your weaknesses and shortcomings can be just another way of saying, 'I don't want responsibility'. Like the man who confesses to be unable to work the washing machine or the woman who declares that she is useless when it comes to fitting a plug to an electrical implement, chances are that you are using your weaknesses to get what you want. In the case of the man who doesn't understand the washing machine, this means that he won't have to deal with the laundry; in the case of the woman who is all thumbs in technical matters, this means that she can delegate any unwanted tasks to someone else. Their intimate level becomes their surface level. Does this mean that underneath they are quite strong? Well, some of them are, considering they get what they want and have other people do all the hard work for them. Whether they are necessarily very happy with it is another question altogether.

In order to develop a positive self-image you will ultimately have to work on the intimate level. No amount of outwardly visible success will ever make up for you not liking yourself or suffering from permanent self-doubt. Once you have sorted out your true feelings, the surface level follows suit. A positive self-image is reflected in the way you act and behave, and it is also reflected in how others feel about you. As you learn to respect yourself, others respect you.

If you feel that your surface level is already quite successful, then this is going to make it a bit easier for you to work on the intimate level. It is always an advantage to perceive that some things are already going right for you because you can build on the positive feeling that others see you as an achiever. If, however, you don't like yourself *and* you feel no one else appreciates you either, the task of improving your self-image seems that much harder because you don't really know what you are trying to achieve. Some people will be able to look back at a modest number of achievements; others have had many successes. Curiously enough it is not the amount of success you have had that will make you happy, it is whether you *acknowledge* what you have accomplished that will determine how good you feel about yourself. Satisfaction depends on whether you are able to *recognize* your success, and whether your success has any meaning to you.

WHAT ARE YOU LOOKING FOR?

If you want to improve anything in your life, it makes sense to be specific about what exactly it is you want to improve. The more general your aim, the less likely you are to hit your target. Which areas of your life need improvement? Which aspects of your personality stop you from making the most of each day? What is it you

lack to make you happy? No, the correct answer to this
last question is not 'a partner who loves me'! Whatever
is lacking is lacking inside yourself, not in the outside
world.

When you look closely at yourself you will find that,
on the whole, you are not altogether without confidence,
self-love or peace of mind. We all have a certain amount
of these qualities; in fact we often have quite a lot of
these valuable assets, *but not in the areas where we want
them*. We may be perfectly confident talking to other
people, but the moment we find someone attractive, we
clam up. Or we may find it easy to speak our mind in
the office, but when we are with friends we dare not say
anything because we are afraid of losing their respect. Or
we may be painfully honest when we look at our own
faults but evasive when we look at other people's shortcomings, which can ultimately lead to a situation where
everyone else appears to be better than we are. You can
possess a certain quality and apply it in one situation
but not in another, with the result that although the
quality is there, you act as if you didn't possess it at all.
This situation has its positive aspects, however, because
if you already have a strength in one area you only need
to *transfer* it to another, rather than create that strength
from scratch.

SHIFT YOUR PERSPECTIVE

Changing your perspective is probably the hardest
change to make if you want to improve your self-image.
Once you have been thinking negatively about yourself
for a while it becomes a habit, and as soon as a situation
arises that taxes your self-esteem you react accordingly.
It is like having an old record playing inside you with a
song that goes, 'You can't do it, and if you could you
wouldn't deserve the success'. And even though you
don't like the record, it seems to be set off automatically
whenever you want to succeed or make any constructive
changes to your life.

In order to change your perspective from negative to

positive, you need to throw out that old record and, figuratively speaking, replace it with a friendlier one. A good way to get rid of the old 'song' is to look at it carefully and find out who gave you that record in the first place, because the chances are that you didn't put it there yourself. Disparaging internal messages often go back to your last relationship or even as far back as childhood. If you hear every day that you are useless or clumsy or unlovable, you will eventually believe it, whether the statement was true in the first place or not. Everyone can be brainwashed into having low self-esteem; it is just a matter of time. Once the record has been firmly installed in your subconscious mind, it goes on playing, even if the original 'donor' has long gone. When a husband treats his wife with condescension, after a while she will begin to feel unworthy. When a wife puts her husband down day in day out, he will begin to lose self-esteem – unless he puts a halt to her behaviour.

People can stay trapped in an untenable relationship because they believe those negative messages they get from their partner. As they begin to feel more and more worthless, they become more hesitant to leave the relationship because they believe no one else would want them. In this way, a vicious circle is established whereby their lack of confidence keeps them in a situation that makes them unhappy. This is even worse for a child who is entirely dependent on his or her parents and cannot just walk out when life at home is unacceptable.

Sit down for a little while and make the effort of tracing back your negative record. Where have you heard these failure messages before? When did they start? Can you remember a time when you felt better about yourself?

The reason why it can be helpful to look for the person who 'gave' you the record is that, with hindsight, you will be able to discover what their motives were. Have you ever thought about why someone has to put others down? Only people who feel insecure and don't like themselves need to belittle others. When you feel a failure, you feel unhappy, and for some people the only relief from these negative feelings is to make others feel even worse, particularly if those other people show any promise or ambition. The humiliator desperately needs to bolster his or her ego by wielding power over others, be it emotionally or physically.

A common fallacy is to believe that if someone treats you badly it is because there is something wrong with you. The truth is that the person who humiliates or abuses others is the one who has something wrong with them, not their victim. When you look back over old memories where you were belittled by another person, try to see the scene as an outside observer who watches a film on a screen. This will enable you to look at the event from a different angle and, above all, from an adult perspective. It will now be a lot easier to say that it was *not* all your fault, and that maybe the other person had their own reasons why they couldn't bear to see you successful or happy.

The reason why I recommend this review of the past is that your ability to discard the old record will depend on its credibility. If you feel that the old messages are valid and true, you will want to keep the record. If, however, you can pick holes in it, if it no longer stands up to scrutiny, you will find it easier to get rid of it.

NEW FOR OLD

Let us assume that you have managed to discredit the old messages, or that you have merely decided that you don't want them any more. The next question is, where do you get your new record from? It is essential to fill in the space where the old message was, otherwise it becomes too easy for the old thought patterns to re-establish themselves.

Basically, your new record can contain any message you want, which of course opens the way for breath-taking options. There are, however, a few rules you should observe (these are described in more detail in *Positive Thinking*).

Be positive and concise

Your new message should be phrased positively and
concisely. Here are a few examples: I am taking control
and making my own decisions; I am valuable and
deserve to have the best possible life; I solve problems
confidently and easily; I am calm and collected as I go
through life successfully.

Practise regularly

In order to establish a new thought pattern, you need
to practise it regularly. Initially, this will have to happen
on a conscious level. You will have to repeat your positive thoughts deliberately, ten to twenty times a day over
a period of at least two to three weeks until the message
becomes instilled subconsciously and starts appearing in
your mind automatically.

Use your imagination

Spend time imagining what it will be like once you start
feeling positive about yourself. Imagine that one night,
while you are asleep, a miracle happens and, on waking
up the next morning, you feel confident and good about
yourself. How would you know that things had
changed? In what ways would you behave differently?
What sort of things would you start doing that you could
not do before? What things could you stop doing which
you never wanted to do in the first place? And above all,
how would other people know that you had changed?

Keep trying

Let me warn you – you will feel strange repeating these
new thoughts to yourself. You will feel vaguely ridiculous and on the brink of abandoning your ego-boosting
project, but please don't! All new ideas seem peculiar to
start off with, simply because you are not used to them.

It is the same with a new pair of shoes – until you have worn them in they feel a bit uncomfortable; so you can either throw them away or keep wearing them until they fit.

SELF-RESPECT STARTS AT HOME

It is quite surprising how much influence our outward appearance has on the way we feel about ourselves. A new dress, a new suit or a new hairstyle can actually lift our spirits because they make us feel more attractive. This is, without a doubt, one of the reasons why many women use make-up – it makes them feel better to know that they look good.

The way you present yourself, your appearance and looks, all say something about your attitude towards yourself. Feeling that other people will have to like you as you are is all well and good, but the question is, do *you* like how you are? When you look in the mirror, are you happy with what you see?

When you feel miserable you tend to neglect your outward appearance. You cannot be bothered to spend any time on improving your looks because you are too busy feeling unhappy. The usual argument at this stage is to say that you will think about your looks once you feel better, but why not make the effort to improve your appearance in order to give yourself a boost of confidence? It is true that if you feel good about yourself, you are automatically more interested in your appearance, but it also works the other way round.

In my practice as an analytical hypnotherapist I sometimes give clients (female *and* male) 'homework' to do and ask them to improve their appearance in one way or another, and when I see them for the next session, a much happier person walks through my door, more hopeful and confident that they will find a solution to their problems.

Being well-groomed does not mean you have to go out and buy expensive clothes. What it does mean is that you look after yourself, which makes a statement to yourself and everyone around you. You are saying that you consider yourself *worth* the effort it takes to look good, and that is already half the battle in developing a more positive self-image.

DEVELOPING NEW SOCIAL SKILLS

As we have seen in previous interviews, there exists a considerable difference between the way some people feel when they are at a social gathering with a partner and by themselves. Being solo shifts the focus of attention on to you, and this means that you need to take responsibility for your own social success or failure. There is no one else to whom you can pass the buck. A partner can be useful because you can hide behind him or her, tagging along in their shadow, letting them do all the talking. This may be a bit boring but a lot safer than exposing yourself to the scrutiny of a group.

There are many ways of hiding behind someone else, just as there are certain social attitudes that help make you invisible. One such attitude is to refer to someone as 'Brian's girlfriend' or 'Anita's husband', or, as is the custom in the United States, to address the wife by her husband's full name, for example Mrs John Rogers. It makes you wonder how Denis Thatcher would feel about being referred to as Mr Margaret Thatcher . . .

There is not a lot we can do about societal peculiarities, but we can certainly work on our own attitude. Having lived as someone else's adjunct does not make that task particularly easy, but it can be done, provided you are prepared to put some effort into it. Those interviewed who had worked on their confidence and social skills reported that they could not believe the positive difference it made to their life. As one lady put it, 'There is nothing like feeling a person in your own right!'

At the same time, the interviewees also agreed that initially they had had grave doubts as to their chances of success. Many felt very worried at presenting themselves as singles in social contexts where before they had appeared as part of a couple, and quite a few of them

confessed to being exhausted with nervous tension when
faced with going to an event on their own. However,
with experience the anxiety wore off, more or less
quickly, depending on the individual disposition. Several
interviewees even found that, to their own surprise, they
actually *preferred* going to social events on their own;
they felt less hampered and more 'themselves'.

Communication is the basis of all successful socializing.
This does not mean you have to be the fastest talker
or the one with the most interesting job or hobbies.
Communication takes place on a multitude of levels. It
embraces skills such as listening just as much as talking,
and these skills can be applied in *any* situation, be it at
an informal get-together, at your department's Christmas
party in an expensive restaurant, or the local dog-breed-
ers annual show. Wherever people get together, certain
ground rules apply. Once you understand them you can
apply them anywhere and know that you will be successful.

LISTENING COUNTS

'I don't like going to parties. I never know what to say.'
It is true to say that, in order to have a good time, you
will need to participate when you are with a group.
Therefore, the erroneous assumption is that the person
who talks most and laughs loudest is having the best
time. However, communication is a bipolar affair. It takes
both a speaker *and* a listener to make a conversation
successful. If everyone were to talk all the time, no one
would be particularly happy. The joy of relating a story
is having an attentive audience.

A good listener can be the most popular person in a
group. People feel drawn to a quiet person, *provided their
calmness comes across as interest in what the other person is
talking about*. It is therefore not advisable to scrutinize
your fingernails or stare at the wallpaper while the other
person is speaking, but neither is it necessary to have
eye-contact all the time. It is often easier to take something in while you are looking away from your partner

occasionally, in the same way as you don't look at someone all the time while you are talking to them. Next time
you observe a conversation between two people, watch
out for the frequency of eye contact as they are talking
and listening respectively.

There is a difference between 'active' listening and
what I call 'empty' listening. Some people just fire a
number of questions at you, and before you have fin-
ished your answers, they launch into the next lot. These
people are not really taking in what you are saying, and
they often leave you with the feeling that you have been
interrogated or tested. This kind of listening is 'empty'
because it is not meaningful. When someone is listening
'actively' to you they integrate the information they are
receiving from you into their own experiences. An active
listener will therefore make sure he understands what
the other person is talking about, and if he doesn't, he
will ask questions or offer assumptions of how he views
the matter, letting the other person correct him if necessary. If you want to learn something from what you
have heard, you may have to speak a little bit as well
as listen.

Every speaker needs some reaction from their
audience. 'Oh really?' is nice, but not activating or
encouraging. A good listener gets into the speaker's
framework and shows that he is trying to understand
the subject matter.

However, not everything you are listening to is going
to be interesting, and you certainly have the right to be
selective as to what person you want to make a special
effort for. There is no need to subject yourself to a thirty-
minute monologue of gossip about people you don't
know (unless you enjoy listening to these kind of tales
of course). Just because you are not an accomplished
conversationalist yourself does not mean you have to put
up with other people's verbal rubbish. Exposing yourself
to negative talk is disheartening and uncomfortable, so
expose yourself to it as little as possible on a voluntary
basis. We all go through times with friends or relatives
where there are arguments and misunderstandings. This
is inevitable and we cannot avoid it. There is, however,
no need to subject yourself to unpleasant conversations

in your spare time, for example at a party. If you get stuck with someone who speaks in a derogatory way about others, or who boasts, or who complains incessantly about their lot in life, find a way of walking away. Listening to lamentations and unpleasantness has no educational value. Find those people who are positive and are worth listening to!

QUALITY NOT QUANTITY

People who have communication problems often say that they feel they are not well enough informed about current affairs to join in when there is a general discussion. They are afraid that they have nothing interesting or worthwhile to contribute, and they are worried that they will sound stupid and lose face in front of others.

Indeed, it would be foolhardy to talk about something you know nothing about, just for the sake of saying something. However, you can still offer an opinion, even if you are not quite sure. It is all a matter of how you put it. Rather than presenting your view as a fact, you may want to put it as a question. 'Isn't it country X's internal financial difficulties that are causing the problems?' is a more cautious approach than, 'Of course, country X is in great financial difficulties!' Bluffing is fine if you have the nerve, but it can get really embarrassing if someone turns around and asks, 'What financial difficulties?' and you can't reply because you only got your information from a quick glance at a paper's headline. If, on the other hand, you make it clear by the way you phrase your opinion that you don't consider yourself an expert on the subject, you not only make a contribution to the conversation, but you also stimulate it. As there are usually a few others in the group who are better informed, they will be quite ready to fill you in – and before you know it, you've learned something new.

On the whole, it appears that men feel more competent when it comes to current affairs and business, whereas women are more confident in psychological matters like relationships, emotions and personal affairs. This is possibly because there is still a difference in the way boys and girls are brought up. Even though times have changed, girls are still encouraged to develop the caring, pleasing aspects of their personality, whereas boys are educated to become providers and practical (and, if necessary, tough) negotiators with the outside world. This may account for the different interests men and women take later on in life and, of course, if you are interested in a subject you are more likely to apply yourself to it and become knowledgeable, which in turn makes you more confident in conversations.

It is a good idea to make an effort to start reading the newspapers again, and not just the television page. Being familiar with current political and social issues will help you participate more confidently in general conversations that arise when you are, for example, at a party where you don't know anyone.

Don't forget that when you are on your own you need to get out and about in order to have your share of human contact. In order to make your outings enjoyable, you want to feel successful, and one way of achieving this is to make sure you have something to say. The more interests or hobbies you have, the easier it is.

But what if you are shy? You may feel that you have something to say but you are just not used to talking about yourself or your interests. Consequently when someone asks you a question about yourself you answer in one little sentence and then withdraw again into your shell. The problem with this approach is that it creates an awkward silence and a break in the conversation. It makes you sound surly and unforthcoming, and the other person can easily feel that they have trespassed on to forbidden territory.

There is a simple thing you can do to prevent this situation arising. Whenever you reply, make it your rule to answer in more than one sentence. Let me give you some example dialogues, together with the perceived meaning your answer has to the listener. Let us assume someone addresses you at a get-together:

X: 'And how do you know our host?'
You: 'From work'.

['I'm not interested in talking to you. Your question is boring.']
Much better would be the following:
X: 'And how do you know our host?'
You: 'We work together at Jenners'. He's in accounts and I'm in marketing.'
['It's nice of you to take an interest in me. I'm glad we can have a bit of a chat.']
Or another example:
X: 'Have you seen the latest Woody Allen?'
You: 'Yes.'
['Yes, but I don't really feel like discussing it with you.']
Much better would be the following:
X: 'Have you seen the latest Woody Allen?'
You: 'Yes, but I didn't particularly like it. I thought it was too long. What did you think?'
['Yes, and I'm pleased to be able to discuss it with you and interested to discover how you found it.']

By being just a little bit more specific in your answer you are signalling to the other person that you are taking them seriously and consider them worthy of an extended reply; in other words, you encourage the continuation of the conversation.

When you don't know anyone at a party, it can be a bit of a struggle to get going in conversation, especially if your boredom threshold is low. But don't forget that small talk has its advantages. It allows you to look people over, observe how they speak and behave, and get a general first impression. Also, it makes sense to stay with everyday topics until you know someone better.

People tend to be cautious about what they reveal about themselves when they meet you for the first time – hence the talk about the weather and the latest political news. An exception is the stranger-on-the-train phenomenon, the old lady who tells you all about herself on the journey from London to Bournemouth. It is different if you know you won't see the other person again. . . .

Improving your conversational skills is a matter of practising active listening and being receptive, but also of participating as a speaker. If you concentrate on the listening and work on your more-than-one-sentence replies, you are well on your way to becoming a good communicator.

MAKING OTHERS FEEL COMFORTABLE

When you entertain at your house or when you invite a friend to stay, there are a few methods of ensuring that your guests feel at ease.

As the host or hostess, you are the only one who knows all your guests, so it is your task to make sure that people get to know one another as quickly as possible. It is wise to try to avoid having a bunch of people standing around your living room who don't know what to say to one another.

As your guests arrive, pick those who are easy-going and extrovert and introduce them to someone else by giving a bit of information about each. For example: 'Helen, this is Miranda Dixon who used to work with me when I was still at Beechams. And this is Helen Smith who I met when we were on the same ward when I had my appendix out last year.'

What you are doing is facilitating the start of a conversation between those two ladies. They now each have a snippet of background information which can easily lead to further questions or comments. Once everyone in the room is engaged in conversation, the atmosphere becomes more relaxed, and any new arrivals are greeted by a welcoming din which makes them feel they are joining a group of people who are having a good time. After a while you may want to go round and check that no one feels left out or stands about on their own. When you have guests who are particularly shy you can help by spending some time talking to them to draw them out a bit before you introduce them to someone else.

However, don't be overkeen with your introductions. I once observed a hostess who, disregarding an ongoing conversation, interrupted the speaker in the middle of a sentence to drag him off and introduce him to someone else. She did the same thing with another couple of people, until she finally met her match. The gentleman she had interrupted firmly disentangled his arm from her grip and told her that he was in the middle of a conversation with someone and wished to continue it.

The smaller you keep the number of guests, the more

opportunity you will have to have a good time yourself.
When there are many people to look after you can spend
the whole evening racing about making sure everyone
has enough to eat and drink and is happily chatting to
someone else.

The situation is very different when you have just one
guest. On a one-to-one basis, attention is ensured at all
times, although this makes the occasion more intense. If
you are getting on well together, it makes the visit even
better, but if you have nothing to say to one another,
the situation is far worse than it would be in a group
where there are a number of people to choose from
should you not like the one to whom you are talking.
Initially it may be advisable to make the visit a short
one; for example, tea in the afternoon or a drink in the
evening. If you are worried about the situation, you can
always indicate that you will have to go out at a certain
time and thereby set a time limit to the visit.

Of course you will want to look after your visitor and
offer him or her a nice meal or whatever is appropriate
for the time of day. This is fine; just make sure you don't
go overboard with your preparations. It can be a bit
overpowering when you are invited for tea and find that
your host has weighed down the table with gateaux,
cakes and biscuits. Put yourself in your visitor's shoes –
you begin to feel doubtful whether you could ever return
the invitation because you could not offer such a variety
of culinary goodies.

Think about it – what is it that makes you feel at
ease when you are invited somewhere, the food or the
company? When the conversation is interesting, you
don't really notice what you are eating, whereas if you
are bored, your most likely thought would be, 'Well, at
least the food was good.' Food takes a secondary role,
unless it is exceptionally good or bad.

Another mistake to avoid is to spend a long time in
the kitchen while your visitor is there. Preparations
should take place beforehand so that you can dedicate
your attention wholeheartedly to your guest. After all,
there is a reason why you have picked that particular
person to visit you, that reason being that you like them
or would like to make friends with them. Make sure this

comes across in the way you deal with their visit. The more comfortable your guest is, the more comfortable you feel, and with every successful visit your confidence will grow further.

MAKING FRIENDS

Once you have left school or university, once you have settled into a permanent job, the rate at which you make friends tends to drop. As you settle into a professional routine, you tend to see the same faces every day.

As a youngster, there are generally more opportunities to get to know new people. In a way, you can't avoid meeting and getting to know others as you go through your school years. There are many opportunities to make friends as you work in groups together, go on school outings together and do the same sports as others. Also, other children in the neighbourhood are potential new friends, and if you have cousins of about your own age whom you see regularly, this adds even further opportunities.

However, even though there are usually plenty of occasions when you can become friendly with others, not every child will do so. Shyness can prove to be a stumbling block, for example when a child cannot approach others and is therefore not noticed or, even worse, is bullied. When such a child spends most of his schooldays away from home at a boarding school, it can have the most severe consequences for his ability to form relationships later on in life. Unless they are able to fit into a group of peers successfully, children can become desperately lonely, and if their calls for help are ignored or dismissed by their parents, the consequences can be very serious indeed, and the child will go into adult life with a sense of social failure.

Later on in life, possibilities to meet new people diminish in that they no longer present themselves automatically. Unless you actively seek to meet others, for example by going out, joining clubs, going to classes etc, you can easily lose contact with the outside world. For many people, colleagues at work are their main social contact apart from their partner. Once the partner is no longer there, or if relationships at work are unsatisfactory, the social network can easily break down.

Apart from the fact that you need friends to give your life variety and to help you to see other people's points of view, friends are also indispensable as support systems. When you leave home, you need to build a reliable social network, a social 'family'. Even the most independent person needs others with whom they can share their experiences and feelings, and who will give them recognition and confirmation of their worth.

When people enter into a relationship with a partner, friendships are often neglected, at least initially. After a while, when the person has settled into a steady relationship with their partner, friendships are taken up again because they provide a counterbalance to the relationship, an outside point of reference so to speak.

Neglecting or abandoning your friendships because of a relationship is unwise because friendships have one big advantage over relationships – they are non-sexual and don't require you to spend most of your time together. This makes for less strain and therefore more goodwill between friends. Both parties have to compromise less than in a sexual relationship and, because they can be themselves, each feels more at ease with the other.

Even though friendships lack the physical aspect of relationships, they are an important source of emotional closeness and, as such, can have a stabilizing effect on your psyche. This is why I consider reliable friendships to be one of the fundamental requirements for happiness as a single.

In this context, it is important to understand what makes a friendship work and how to win new friends, but it is equally essential to be a good friend yourself. The following pages will introduce ideas of how to go about making friends and making friendships work. The strategies are very much the same as those for successful relationships, so your knowledge will prove useful should you choose to go into another relationship.

Close friendships are still more common in women

than they are in men, at least in heterosexual men. It is also more common for women to speak about feelings and discuss them with friends than it is for men who seem to derive their sense of worth from professional achievements rather than from interpersonal relationships. This is not to say that men don't want or need friendships, but they certainly don't concentrate their efforts on them as do women. I therefore expect that some male readers will struggle a bit more with this chapter and even feel somewhat reluctant to take on board the ideas presented. However, why not look at new concepts every once in a while? You never know, they may open a new world to you. . . .

TRUST YOUR FEELINGS

When you meet new people, you tend to have an instinctive reaction to them. There are some people whom you dislike practically instantly, others to whom you feel quite close even though you have only just met them. Whether you call it 'vibes' or 'chemistry', the fact remains that an irrational process takes place the moment you set eyes on another person. This subconscious reaction is different from prejudices or preconceptions, both of which are triggered off by a combination of past experiences and present needs.

As much as we would all like to be open-minded about others, we nevertheless have certain expectations of what our friends should look like, how they should dress and behave and what should be their general attitude towards life. The more of these aspects we have in common with someone, the more likely it is that we will choose them as friends.

When we meet someone for the first time, our preconceived ideas come to the fore instantly and we start putting the other person into a particular category in our minds. He or she is 'conservative' or 'liberal', 'unconventional' or 'straight-laced', 'shrewd' or 'naïve', and so on. These categories have evolved throughout the years of our childhood and adolescence, and even though the

categories are changed, moderated or extended as time
goes by, this will not happen quickly. This means that
at any given point in time we have a fairly clear picture
of what qualities a friend should have.

Some issues will, of course, be more important than
others. How compatibility is assessed differs from person
to person. You may not care much for a person's way
of dressing, but this may be outweighed by their loyalty
and warm-heartedness; or you may be prepared to put
up with someone's unpunctuality because you know that
they are emotionally reliable and always ready to support
you. Some people find the use of slang unacceptable;
others find it amusing and don't really mind it. Your
priorities are the sum total of your personality. There is
not much point in forcing yourself to accept something
that goes against the grain. If another person's idiosyncrasies make you feel tense or nervous, for whatever
reason, then you won't open up to them. Frankness and
trust, however, are two of the main ingredients
of friendship; without them, the relationship cannot
possibly be satisfactory for you. In this respect,
preconceptions are useful because they provide you with
criteria that will help you to select your potential friends.
You cannot be friends with everyone; you have to have
a reference point within yourself that you can go by, and
this reference point consists of your feelings and your
needs.

Preconceptions are different from prejudices in that
they are more flexible. When you are prejudiced, you
have made up your mind once and for all that a certain
category of person is not to be trusted and therefore not
to be allowed into your life; in other words, you will not
even consider looking at an individual member of that
category or judging them on their personal merits to
check whether your prejudice is justified. In fact, many
prejudiced people have never even met anyone from the
group to which they so strongly object. Their judgement
is usually mainly derived from hearsay. This is a shame
because they unnecessarily narrow down the number of
potential new friends.

When I suggest that you should trust your feelings
when you meet someone new, I would also like you to

listen to your intuition. We often pick up signals subconsciously which may well seem to contradict what we perceive logically. Outwardly, a person may be everything we like, and yet inwardly we can feel an undercurrent of resistance and distrust when we encounter them. It is like a warning signal coming on which seems totally irrational. Trust your sixth sense, it is always right. It rarely happens that you react strongly against someone, but when you do, take heed and don't let yourself be confused by logical rationalizations. If you have a bad feeling about someone, it makes sense to listen to it; it is unlikely that this feeling is unfounded.

BE SELECTIVE

Whether you are single or not, don't drop your standards when it comes to the people with whom you surround yourself. Check through your existing circle of friends. Are there some from whom you dread getting a phone call? Are there some that only come to see you when they want something? Are there people who constantly complain that you never come to see them, but never make any efforts to come and see you? In other words, are there people who make you feel uncomfortable or annoyed every time you are with them?

This again is a matter of listening to your feelings. What is the point of continuing to associate with people who make you feel negative? Pessimistic people around you will depress you and the more you see of them, the greater will be their negative influence on you. Bad company is *not* better than no company at all, so keep up your standards.

The way to find out whether someone is good for you or not is simply to close your eyes and imagine being with that person. Now pay attention to what is happening with your emotions. Does it make you angry to think of them, even though there has not been a row with them lately? Do they show interest in you and in how you are getting on? Do they make you feel wanted? If you have to say 'no' to the last two questions, you want to check whether this is a recent development or whether the situation has always been like that. If you can't remember it ever having been different, there is not a lot of hope, and you may want to consider discontinuing the connection. If, however, their withdrawal is recent, there is a good chance of rescuing the relationship by addressing the issue and finding out why things have changed for the worse.

The reason why people drop their standards, or have low standards to start with, is unhappiness with themselves. When you don't feel good about yourself, when things go wrong in your life and you cannot cope, when you have just come out of a disastrous relationship, you start to doubt yourself. You begin to scrutinize yourself, your looks, your manners, the way you behave in certain situations, and you start finding fault and putting yourself down. As a consequence, you feel inferior and unworthy, so you put yourself down a bit more, and as this process carries on you begin seriously to lose self-confidence. Once you stop respecting yourself, your standards drop automatically, the reasoning being, 'I'm worthless, therefore nobody can possibly like me, therefore I have to accept what I am given. I can count myself lucky that anyone wants me at all.' When this attitude is a result of a recent split-up, chances are that it will reverse by itself as time goes by. When you are a basically optimistic person, positivity is bound to return in the end.

Standards also have a lot to do with how clearly we perceive our needs. People who come from families where needs were not acknowledged find it more difficult later on in life to appreciate and fulfil their own needs. Let me give you an example. One of my clients, let's call him Thomas, is a young man in his mid-twenties and comes from a large family with five children. His father did not have a lot of time for his family. He worked hard in his business and was a good provider in the material sense, but was incapable of giving emotional support either to his children or to his wife who was very much left to her own devices when it came to running their big family. The father went out of his way to accommodate the wishes of other people but never those of his own family.

The mother, basically a caring but insecure person, tried to cope with the situation by immersing herself in various activities and sports which helped to take her mind off the fact that she had a husband who did not show any affection or interest in her. Knowing that she could not leave her husband without leaving the children behind, she decided to stay until the children were grown up.

Repressing her own needs for love and attention, she indirectly passed on the message to her children. Weaknesses were ridiculed and complaints ignored. Whenever the children expressed any negative feelings or needs, they were punished by sarcasm, contempt or non-acknowledgement, thereby labelling their behaviour as selfish, self-indulgent and exaggerated.

Growing up in this context, Thomas was unaware of his own needs. As he watched what happened to his sisters and brothers when they expressed their wishes, he realized that there was not much point in doing so himself because the wishes would be ignored anyway. He consequently proceeded to do the same thing his mother was doing – he suppressed his own needs. He could not sustain an interest in any hobbies he started, and life became meaningless and depressing. No one had ever shown an interest in him, and now he could not take an interest in himself. His relationships with others consisted of shallow friendships where he could not give of himself and did not allow himself to accept love from others. He was happiest when he could help others, just like his father had been. As he could not allow himself to fulfil his own needs, he channelled his energies towards other people, helping them solve their problems, and this constituted the only glimpses of contentment in his life.

Another side-effect of his upbringing was that Thomas did not know what he wanted. As he had been taught to ignore his feelings, he did not have a gauge whereby he could measure his likes and dislikes. In other words, he could not develop his own personal standards and felt helpless and confused whenever he had to make any choices in life.

Standards are very personal things; they can never be objective. It is your responsibility to take seriously the needs you feel and to see to their fulfilment by expressing them. This can be done in various ways, and here are some tips to help you on your way.

Be honest with yourself

Acknowledge your own feelings, and not just the good ones. It is easy to sweep negative feelings under the carpet. No one likes them very much; but ignoring them is not going to make them go away.

Express your feelings

You can do so in a quiet and pleasant manner; there is no need to be aggressive or loud. The sooner you talk about what you feel is wrong, the less likely it is that you will lose your temper. Let off steam regularly and you won't have a huge explosion.

Reassess your friendships

When your needs are constantly disregarded by someone around you, you may want to consider loosening the ties with that person or even ending the friendship. A relationship which frequently makes you unhappy is not good for you. It may sound difficult to break off an unsatisfactory relationship, but it is even harder to live with one.

Value your life

Understand that you are unique and valuable and that this is the only life you have. Make it as beautiful as you can and surround yourself with people who really like

you. You deserve to enjoy life and to have the best there
is.

Set realistic standards

Make sure that the standards you set for yourself are
not disproportionately higher or lower than those you
set for others. If you are willing to find excuses for
other people's shortcomings, you will also have to allow
weaknesses in yourself. This also applies the other way
around; if you demand excellence from others, you will
have to strive for perfection yourself.

LOOK AFTER YOUR FRIENDSHIPS

Just as you want to reassess those relationships that don't
come up to your standards, you need to attend to those
you want to keep. Like any other relationship, you will
have to work at friendships so that they can grow and
thrive. If you neglect them, they wither. This does not
mean that you need to be together all the time. On the
contrary, excessive closeness can become stifling unless
you can be very relaxed with one another.

Looking after a friendship means keeping in touch and
communicating. It doesn't really matter whether this is
once a week or once a year; it is quality that counts, not
quantity. When you just sit back and let the other person
make all the arrangements, you create an imbalance
where your friend puts more into the relationship than
you do. This tends to work for a while, but at some
point your friend will become frustrated with this one-
sidedness. By being passive in a relationship you are
giving off a signal, and that signal is that you are not
really interested. Would *you* want to continue a relationship where you received this sort of signal? Put yourself
into your friend's shoes – it feels discouraging, doesn't
it? It is not enough to ensure that the other person enjoys
your company when you get together if you never take
any active steps to promote your meetings.

There has to be a balance between give and take. When the chemistry is right, this usually happens automatically, and this is the best and least complicated way. Still, it can happen that one of you is particularly stressed or feeling down for some reason, in which case it is necessary for the other one to take the initiative for a while *without expecting to get rewarded for it by way of attention*. If a friend is upset about something, your support is needed immediately. You may have to take the initiative over a prolonged period of time until he or she feels better again. You do not have to take over your friend's life, but you should keep in touch, showing that you are available to discuss the situation, that you are willing to encourage and give moral support to help your friend get on his or her feet again. While this is going on, your friend may be too distressed to enquire about *your* problems and *your* well-being, but the balance will redress itself after a while.

Going through difficult times together brings friends closer and strengthens relationships, provided each feels they can lean on the other whenever necessary. In order to reach this point, there has to be a sense of trust and openness between you which will gradually evolve over time. It makes sense to be careful about who you confide in, but as you get to know the other person better, you need to allow them to see not just your public self, but also your inner self, otherwise the relationship will get stuck on a superficial level. If you spend your time talking about all the things you have achieved in your life, the relationship will not go beyond a merely social level. It is simply not true to make out that you don't have problems occasionally or that your successes are delivered without effort. To pretend you are one hundred per cent competent all the time is not only untrue but it will also make you seem daunting to others. Nothing alienates people as easily as someone who seems to operate on a superior level. The display of excellence without a sign of human weakness discourages others to admit to their shortcomings. In order to have a close friendship the other person needs to feel that you are human, otherwise he or she will feel inadequate and less ready to open up to you.

We tend to approach one another cautiously. As our partner reveals something about themselves, we let down our barriers a bit more, which then encourages the other person to proceed in the same way until, bit by bit, we discover the 'real' person in the other one, and they discover who we really are.

Once both sides have revealed their private selves, trust accumulates and strengthens the friendship. At this stage, both parties are emotionally involved in the relationship in a sense where they feel they can be themselves, with all their faults, and still be liked – and, in return, like the other person for allowing them this freedom.

Of course, friendships don't run smoothly all the time. There may be misunderstandings, quarrels and uncertainties about loyalties as the friendship progresses. It is easy to dismiss these hiccups and just sweep them under the carpet – please don't! If you are serious about this relationship you will have to talk about the problem. Many disagreements are a result of irrational assumptions, and if you want to sort things out, you have to speak about them.

People are often afraid or even terrified of tackling unpleasant subjects for fear of being rejected or finding out something they would rather not know. They will often postpone addressing that fearsome topic until it is too late, when the differences have been blown out of all proportion and the friendship is ruined altogether.

It is unpleasant having to admit that your friendship is on the rocks, but it is far more unpleasant to live with this knowledge and not do anything about it. The sooner you tackle the discord, the shorter the time you worry and suffer.

Get together with your friend and discuss the situation. Don't accuse, don't remonstrate, just explain your side, how you are feeling, and ask them to help you dissolve the problem. Don't forget that the person to whom you are speaking is important to you and deserves the opportunity to explain if there has been a misunderstanding or to put right a mistake they may have made.

A good friendship is priceless and it is worth looking after it, not just during the easy times but also when the

going gets tough. Part of your 'maintenance' task is to
be helpful but also honest when you feel unhappy about
the way things are going. If your friend does not know
that you are discontented, they cannot change the situation. Make sure you are open, in a gentle way, so that
the matter can be cleared up and the relationship has a
chance to get back into balance again.

Similarly, if you are on the receiving end of such a
discussion, please bear in mind that your friend is
making a special effort to clear up a problem and that
you need to take this effort seriously and to appreciate
that you have a friend who has the courage to speak out
when things seem wrong.

BEING AT HOME WITHIN YOURSELF

When you have just come out of a relationship, no matter
whether it ended amicably or tragically, you feel lost.
You feel as if you were living in a house that was the
right size for two people but far too big for one. You
feel empty inside but at the same time churned up by
all sorts of contradictory feelings like sadness, anger, fear
and pain. These feelings can even result in physical pain,
similar to withdrawal symptoms.

When you get involved with another person, you let
them into your life. You share your time with them,
and as a consequence, you build up a mutual fund of
experiences and memories; in other words, you create a
space inside yourself, restricting your own wishes and
needs to a certain extent to accommodate a very special
person in your life. It is this very space that was occupied
by your partner that is now so painfully empty. Even
just *imagining* a partner, if you have never had one, can
create this void and yearning inside, almost as if you
had vacated a nice room in your house and cannot find
a tenant to move in.

The trick is to begin to fill these empty spaces inside
with yourself, to expand over a greater area and re-
possess what was yours in the first place.

Interestingly, there seems to be a difference between

men and women when it comes to the emotional space they allow someone else to take up. Whereas women are quite willing to restrict their own domain at the cost of repressing their own needs, men tend, figuratively speaking, to put women into an annexe. Men are far less ready to have their space restricted by the presence of another person. This does not mean that they are not sad when the woman 'moves out', but there is a greater tendency in men to keep a partner at arm's length emotionally.

With the women's liberation movement there has been a drift towards greater independence for women, both on the financial and the emotional side. As men still largely hold the power financially and politically, many women wish to reach those same positions of power to ensure greater equality between the sexes and greater respect for women in particular. On the surface, this looks like a noble pursuit. Surely, everyone must be for equality?

But stop for a moment and consider what this has meant in real terms for many of the women who are in powerful positions today. In order to attain power, women have generally had to become like men emotionally – tough and abstract, and repressing their feelings. If this were to continue, we would end up with not just half the population negating their own feelings and unable to experience intimacy and commitment, but the *entire* population. What a price to pay for power! Is it really worth it?

In the rest of this section I will discuss why our feelings are of such great importance to our happiness and why it would make more sense for there to be a men's liberation movement that teaches how to accept and express your feelings so that men need no longer fight for power at the expense of women. It would be a great mistake if women tried to follow in men's footsteps and never fully realized the strength and potential of their own feminine qualities which are now gradually starting to be recognized and encouraged as extremely valuable in some organizations. Without feelings, for example, all that is left is deadly meaninglessness inside.

YOUR FEELINGS ARE YOUR STRENGTH

Showing your feelings, or even admitting to having feelings, is still considered a weakness, particularly amongst men. As a result, women are considered the weaker sex, because they are the ones who most commonly display their emotions. But what is it that promotes this myth about feelings being a weakness?

The best way of explaining this is probably by looking at what happens with our feelings as we go through our childhood years. Initially, babies express their feelings in a very direct way. When they are hungry, in pain or uncomfortable, they cry, announcing that something is wrong. As the child grows older, it has to learn to suppress its feelings little by little in order to fit in with the society around it. Fits of anger, refusal to comply with rules and regulations, even noisy exclamations of joy, are frowned upon and often punished or criticized. Consequently, the child learns that its feelings become a stumbling block to the approval of others. The more the child conforms, the fewer difficulties it has in dealing with others. If, however, it insists on making its feelings known, it is rejected or punished. It follows that it does not pay to acknowledge those feelings because they are not acceptable to others. Because expressing feelings gets you into trouble, they start becoming unacceptable to yourself. They make you feel helpless, and because you want to avoid feeling weak, you start pushing back those feelings. As you are now getting on with others more easily, you seem to have done the right thing.

The greater your fear of helplessness, the more energy and determination you must have to suppress and ultimately eliminate it. Compassion and empathy for others have to go; because you are afraid of your own feelings, you need to fight against feelings in others as they keep reminding you of your own. You therefore proceed by treating with contempt all those who show their feelings.

Control is the keyword, rationality and abstract thinking the solution to the anxiety-inducing power of feelings. Striving for power is one way of keeping that anxiety at bay. Being successful becomes compulsory in order to escape a feeling of failure; approval from the outside world is a vital necessity that has to be regained again and again. If you are empty inside you have to attempt to fill the inner void through outside praise and recognition.

Our feelings are important. They are there for a good reason. They constitute a vital part of our self, in fact they *are* our self. If we disregard or ignore our feelings, we are abandoning our inner reality.

In my practice as an analytical hypnotherapist I see the problems this can cause every day. A typical example is when a client feels depressed because of the way they are being treated by their partner or by a parent. When I then begin to ask more specific questions about how they feel about the way they are being treated, the answer is usually, 'My mother can't help it; she has had a difficult childhood,' or, 'My husband is the type who flies off the handle easily. He is under a lot of stress at work.' Note that my question about their feelings has not been answered at all; instead, the client answers by excusing the other person's actions. This is a typical avoidance manoeuvre when you do not want to look at your own feelings. The fear underlying this avoidance is that you would have to admit that you are angry. Such an admission would make you feel guilty because you have learned that it is wrong to think of yourself ('selfish!') and that other people's needs have to come first. This is how other people's feelings can become more important than your own. But as you can't suppress your own emotions altogether, they come out in a different form – the anger becomes internalized and turns into depression.

Feelings are our yardstick, our guideline to reality. If we feel annoyed about something, this feeling is real, no matter what anyone else says. If we feel upset and sad about something, these feelings are real, and we need to deal with them and use them as a guideline for our future actions. When the boss is unreasonable and overloads us with work, there is no point in fuming inside and being nice as pie on the outside. If your behaviour is guided by your feelings then you will have to speak to your boss about the situation. It is not necessary to show your anger in this conversation (although sometimes it helps), but it certainly is necessary to do something about the situation that has caused the anger. In other words, your feelings need to be acknowledged as a warning signal, and then they need to be followed up by appropriate action. As you make constructive use of your negative feelings by acting upon them, you gain control over your life and are therefore in harmony with yourself.

OVERCOMING THE FEAR OF FREEDOM

Isn't it amazing how scary freedom is and how little we do with it when we have it? Think about all the advantages of being on your own. You can go out and come home when you like, you can cook yourself a meal or not, display stubble on your chin without getting comments, leave your place in a mess whenever you feel like it and generally be as uninhibited as you dare. And yet, when we get the opportunity of doing just that, we don't make a lot of use of it. Suddenly, we begin to hanker after a partner, someone who is around us, someone to whom we have to adapt and with whom we have to compromise; in other words, someone who will necessarily restrict our freedom through their mere presence.

What is it then that makes us unable to enjoy and appreciate that time we have to ourselves, and where does this fear of freedom come from?

Quite a few of those interviewed commented that they had had no experience in filling in all that 'empty' time. They had been used to a certain structure, either that of school or university, or that of a marriage or other partnership, so that once the structure had been taken away they felt incapable of erecting their own. They simply didn't know where to start and perceived their new-found freedom as threatening and riddled with feelings of loneliness, doubt and boredom. Rather than take advantage of all the possibilities that presented themselves, they stayed indoors more than previously and generally felt more insecure and anxious, particularly in the first few weeks and months after the break-up of the relationship.

The problem with withdrawing of course is that it makes your fears come true. As you are not active socially, you have less contact with the outside world, you see less of your friends, and therefore you become bored and lonely – and uninteresting. This in turn makes others less keen to approach and, hey presto, your fear has come true – being on your own is horrible.

The truth is that you are creating a lot of this emptiness yourself. Of course I am not talking about a situation where you have just lost your partner because he or she has died or left you. It is only natural that you should miss him or her, especially in the beginning, but the time comes when you need to fill their place with someone or something else. Many people go for the option of finding a substitute partner as quickly as possible so that they don't have to deal with the emptiness that has arisen through their loss. That way they hope to bridge the gap without having to try out new things.

It is true to say that change always has an element of stress in it, for some people more than others. It is quite a drastic situation when you suddenly realize that you are on your own. It is a big step from sharing lots of things with someone else to doing everything on your own. Even those who considered themselves happy singles reported that it took them some time to find their feet and restructure their life and their everyday patterns to new routines. The only difference between the happy singles and the unhappy ones was that the successful singles had believed they would eventually be happy again, whereas the unhappy ones could not even imagine it. What you believe will influence your actions, and your behaviour and actions will eventually make your beliefs come true (see also *Positive Thinking*).

The strategy that seems to work best is to take one day at a time and not waste too much time pondering about a potentially catastrophic future. Most of these imagined disasters never happen anyway, so why fill your head with them? None of us knows what is round the corner. None of us could imagine at one time that we would ever be without our partner, either!

As you begin to live on a day-to-day basis, you can slowly begin to fill your time with enjoyable activities, thereby setting up a structure that is tailored to your needs. You may have to experiment a bit if you are not quite sure what it is you want to do, but that can be quite useful as it will get you in touch with yourself and your needs. It is only too easy to forget about your own needs in a relationship, so you may find that, as a single, you rediscover talents that you haven't put to use in a long time.

You will have to make a lot of decisions all by yourself and you will have to decide to take certain risks ('Will I be too stupid for this evening class?'), but the rewards will be fantastic. As you begin to use the empty times constructively, you shape your own life. This takes courage and determination and is not at all always a straightforward process. At times you might feel that you take two steps forward and one step back, but at least you are going in the direction that *you* choose, making your own way rather than following a path someone else has designed for you. If you leave it to others to run your life, you will have to like what you get. Some people prefer this option because they can blame the other person when things don't work out. If you don't want to take responsibility for yourself, you abdicate your rights. The more you fear freedom, the more readily will you abandon the possibilities of self-determination and choice.

Learning to use freedom constructively is a gradual process. It may be slow, but it certainly helps you build up your strength and confidence, and above all, it gives meaning to your life. As you fill your life with interesting things, you learn to rely on your own abilities and your own judgement, and that is a good feeling.

ALLOW YOURSELF TO BE UNIQUE

People not only worry about using their freedom constructively, they also worry about being different from
others. Man is a herd animal from early on. The ten-
year-old schoolgirl needs to wear a certain type of skirt
in order to feel accepted by her peers; the twelve-year-
old schoolboy gets acutely embarrassed if his mother
turns up at sports day in clothes that set her apart from
the other mothers. And this is how it continues. One
gets a good education, a job, a car, a family and a house.
In extreme cases of adapting to other people, one feels
one needs to keep up with the Joneses and have the
larger car and house and the better paid and higher
status job. The sameness remains, it is only the degree
that varies. The ambition is to leave others behind by
performing better and more successfully, but in the same
field. Only if you stay within the same framework can
you compare your achievements with others and make
it visible to others that you are *better* than they are. This
is not being unique, this is just a refined version of one-
upmanship.

Being different from others is still regarded as negative
or weird. Although we are becoming more tolerant about
unusual sights such as the father rather than the mother
looking after the baby, there is still a slight sense of
reservation at the back of our minds as to whether he is
a 'real' man who can be taken seriously. Equally, we still
have difficulty with other old concepts such as 'fat people
are jolly' or 'black people are less intelligent than white
people'. Both these ideas are nonsense of course but they
usually develop early on and are only eradicated with
difficulty. My five-year-old nephew announced one day
that all girls were stupid. When his mother pointed out
to him that there were quite a few women and girls he
liked, he said, 'Not *them*. Only all the others!' Even
though we see that there are exceptions, we will still
hang on to the original preconception, refusing to let go
of our generalizations.

In a world that is so keen on sameness it takes courage to
be yourself, to set yourself apart from others deliberately.

If it goes well and you are successful with your unusual idea, you are a hero; if it goes wrong, then everyone will shake their heads and say they told you so and point you out to their children as a bad example. Being an outsider is only permissible when you make a lot of money with it. A poor individualist is a weirdo, a rich one is a genius.

To leave the beaten track and follow your own inclinations rather than rely on conventional thinking may sound perilous, but when you come to actually doing it you will find that it isn't. It is the fear of the unknown that conjures up pictures of potential disaster in our minds, and this often prevents us from following our intuition. Instead of listening to that inner voice, we cement rational thought over it and pretend we haven't heard. But it is this inner voice which represents our innermost, unique self and we need to take a lot more notice of it if we want to feel whole.

Those who are lucky enough to follow a vocation in their lives will always have a story to tell of how they first realized that this is what they wanted to do. In fact, we all have a vocation, we all have a place in life which only we can fill, but in order to find out about it we have to have the courage to listen to that inner voice. Courage is needed because the ideas we have often seem unattainable and lead away from everything we have done so far. By following your intuition you may set yourself apart from others, and this is a price that some consider too high to pay for fulfilling their true aims in life.

However, if you can cross that threshold, the rewards are considerable. With a bit of luck, your individuality will fit in with the rest of your life so you don't have to change everything, and with a bit more luck you will even be able to make money with it. But even if you cannot live on your new idea, you will find how much richer you feel in other respects. Only as you recognize your uniqueness and the necessity, at least in some areas of your life, to live that uniqueness, can you fulfil your potential. No one else can live your life and no one else can make your decisions. Your choices are a reflection of your personality. Therefore they cannot be right or wrong – they are simply *your* choice as opposed to anyone else's.

The more you can accept yourself, the easier others will find it to accept you. When you have self-respect, other people will sense it and treat you accordingly; if you behave and think like a victim, you will be treated as one. People know instinctively (here is that inner voice again!) whether they can mess you around or not, simply because you send out signals according to how you feel about yourself.

If you live your life as you think other people want you to live it, you will not feel fulfilled; also, you may find that you misinterpret their wishes. When neither party says what they really want it can easily come to misunderstandings. If everyone is too polite to point out that they are not satisfied, the undesirable situation continues. The longer it goes on, the harder it becomes to say anything, until it is totally impossible to set the matter right without major embarrassment. How much easier to say straight away that you would prefer to do things in a different manner!

In quite a few instances you will have to compromise, but there are enough occasions where no one else is involved and you can make your own decisions, be it changing to a new hairstyle or joining a club or looking for a new job. You can establish your individuality in all sorts of areas, and they don't necessarily all have to be the major areas of your life. Individuality can be expressed through your favourite pastime, and this can help balance out other areas, for example work, where you cannot identify so much with what you are doing. As long as you can create a form of sanctuary for yourself where you can realize your potential and fulfil your needs, you are doing fine.

EXPANDING YOUR BOUNDARIES

Being single, you are in the best position of all to work on your personal and professional development. You can concentrate all your efforts on furthering your career, learning new things and generally having a good time because there is no one else to take into consideration. You are a free agent, and you usually don't appreciate it until you are well into your next relationship. *There is no excuse not to do what you have always wanted to do, it's now or never!* Please don't waste too much time feeling sorry for yourself. You are in the lucky position of being able to immerse yourself in new ventures that will help you push back those boundaries that stop you from growing to your full potential.

It doesn't really matter which area of your life you choose to work on as long as you get started on something. I'm sure that something has already sprung to your mind as you have been reading the first few lines of this chapter. We all have our pet ideas of what we are going to do once we have more time, and not all of them have to do with clearing the kitchen sink or unblocking the loo. We all have those unfulfilled dreams that we have had to keep locked up in the back of our minds, those crazy ideas that we would like to turn into reality if only we had the money or the time or the courage to do so.

Get serious about making them come true! Not all your dreams are too expensive, not all your ideas are too extravagant. Pretend that you mean business this time. Begin to gather information about your project; get prices, locations, facilities that can help you achieve your aim. Don't be discouraged if initially it appears impossible to make your dream come true. There is never just *one* way of going about things – don't look at the wall, look for the doors in the wall. Keep your eyes open for alternatives. Sometimes we are so intent on getting that one particular thing that we overlook another option which may be just as viable.

Working on your own development now is going to pay off in the future. We may not be too keen on having to make the effort of learning Italian irregular verbs, but once we are in Italy we are glad we did. We may have to give up some of our spare time to study for a work-related course, but once we get promoted as a result, we feel good about it. And most of the time it is actually fun to learn a new thing, and this, together with a positive expectation of a successful end result, keeps us motivated to see our project through to the end.

You don't have to choose something 'useful'; development takes place on all levels and in all areas of life. Even though you may go for a new hobby, your involvement will have positive side-effects on other areas. Because you are doing something you enjoy, you are more relaxed, and as you are learning new things, your confidence grows. You will also have something to talk about which can be useful if you are shy and short of topics for conversation with others.

Now let's have a look at what you can do.

WORK-RELATED DEVELOPMENT

It is only too easy to get into a rut professionally, either because you are stuck in a job which does not offer any possibilities for further promotion, or because you find that the type of profession you are in does not suit you. You might have felt vaguely dissatisfied with the situation at work for quite some time, but it is always easier to stay put than to do something about it.

If you have read this far, I'm sure you know what I'm going to say now – if you don't like it, change it. Just because you have made your own bed doesn't mean you have to lie in it forever, and there has never been a better time than right now to deal with the problem. Start making the necessary changes *before* the next relationship comes along; once it does, you won't have either the energy or the inclination to deal with it, at least not for the first year or so.

Take time to sit down and take stock of what your work situation is like. What exactly is it that bothers you? What do you need to do to improve it? Is your boss approachable? Can you raise the issues with him or her? Clarify your situation for yourself, then make it known that there is a problem. Speak to someone who can do something about it. There is no point in complaining to your colleagues; they don't have the authority to change things. It is essential to take serious steps to resolve the problem, otherwise you will become resentful and unhappy. Rather than keeping those feelings down you should regard them as a warning signal telling you it is time to take action.

Once you are clear what the problem is, speak to someone in the company who can do something about it. If, for example, you were promised a promotion a year ago and nothing has happened since, you need to chase it up. This doesn't mean you have to be aggressive, but you will certainly want to find out what the state of affairs is. Have they forgotten or is there another reason why you have not been promoted? If there is another reason you need to know what it is, if only to put your mind at rest that the delay is not due to dissatisfaction with your performance. Ask them to suggest a date when they think the promotion is likely to go through and ask whether it is all right for you to contact them again should nothing happen. This way you show that you are planning to keep a tab on the matter and that you are serious about it. Don't let yourself be fobbed off by vague answers; make sure you understand what you are told. What have you got to lose? They won't sack you for asking questions, will they? And if they did, would you want to work for them anyway?

If your job is all right but going nowhere fast, then this is the time to consider seriously finding another job. Please don't hide behind the excuse that it is not the right time just now – there is no such thing as the right time. You will always be able to find reasons why you can't start looking for another job, but that only adds procrastination to your list of problems rather than solving the original one (see also *Strategies of Optimism*). It takes ten minutes a day to look through the job sections in newspapers, it takes maybe half an hour to update your CV and another half an hour to type it out. In the meantime you can still hang on to your present job, and with the security of a job in the background, you can look at what the market has to offer without being under any financial pressure.

When you feel that you are in the wrong job altogether, you may want to take this opportunity to start thinking seriously about what the alternatives are. Get

information on other professions that appeal to you,
write off for brochures, arrange for chats with people
who know about these professions; *be active!* Training
may be available part-time, in the evenings or as a corre-
spondence course, thus making it possible for you to
keep the old job while you are training. This has the
advantage of enabling you to put some money away
which you may need if you want to become self-
employed afterwards. You may also be eligible for grants
or some other financial support. You can see that there
is a lot of preparatory work to be done. Isn't it lucky
that you have the time to do that now? Through your
situation as a single, you have the opportunity to make
a big step into a more interesting professional future. If
you don't take that opportunity now, when will you ever
take it?

PUT THE SPARKLE BACK INTO YOUR PASTIME

A few weeks ago, I visited my sister in Germany. Going
for a walk, we decided on a route that took us from one
playground to another in order to provide entertainment
for her two sons aged seven and eight. We finally arrived
at a play area which sported a slide in a tube that wound
its way down into a sandpit. In order to get to the top,
you could either walk up some steps or climb up a
pirates' net made of thick ropes. After having tried out
both ways, my nephews decided on the net as being
more fun and henceforth were up and down the net and
the slide like monkeys while my sister and I talked on
a nearby bench. The inevitable happened and one of the
boys came over and asked us to have a go as well.
My sister agreed and went down the slide with them,
confessing afterwards that it was a bit scary inside the
tube when you couldn't see where you were going. Now
the boys insisted on me trying it too. To my surprise I
realized that I wanted to but felt a bit scared. On the
one hand, that pirates' net appealed to me, but at the
same time I was worried about climbing it. At the age

of 37, was I still fit enough to do it? And would I be courageous enough to go down that enclosed slide? I had never really considered all these points when I was watching the children do it, but now that it was my turn I was not so sure I had the courage.

In the end, with a lot of persuasion and encouragement from my nephews, I approached the pirates' net. It was the most peculiar sensation I had had in a long time, climbing up that wobbly construction, having to grip tightly, pull myself up from rung to rung and try to keep my balance all at the same time. Arriving on the last rung, I then had to heave my whole weight on to the platform at the top which turned out to be another stumbling block. Even though I'm only eight stone in weight, I felt about as elegant as a beached whale in attempting this, but in the end I managed.

Now the slide. Again I dithered. Could I do it? *Should* I do it? My younger nephew offered to go first and I could go after him, and this is what we did. As I was sliding down I could feel how I gathered momentum, being pressed against the side of the tube as it went in spirals and curves down to the ground. It actually felt quite nice to whizz down like that!

Having safely arrived feet first in the sandpit I felt absurdly pleased with myself. I had actually done it, and in a strange way it felt really satisfying.

Now I don't suggest for a moment you should go to your nearest playground and, book in hand, race down a slide with the promise that this is the way to make you into a happy person. And yet, you may want to consider some of the thoughts that came to me after my little adventure. I was really amazed at the amount of satisfaction I gained from tackling something that I hadn't done since childhood. Even though the whole incident lasted only a few minutes, I learned that it was the element of exploration that had made it so much fun. It seemed something totally new to do, an experience that differed substantially from what I normally did in my free time. So why not be more adventurous in future? Why only attempt those pastimes that you are reasonably sure you can do? How much more exciting to go for a new challenge, something that gets us away from everyday routine!

Surprise yourself. Do something out of the ordinary, something that sounds crazy but fun. Vary your route from work; get on a double decker bus and stay on it until the end of the line; make a spontaneous phone call to someone you haven't seen in a long time, or better still, pay them a spontaneous visit. If they are not at home, explore the neighbourhood. Visit an auction; see a fortune teller; leave your umbrella at home and go for a walk in the park while it is raining; try out aroma-therapy or foot massage. If you are short of ideas, look through your local paper and see what's on offer. Anything is fine that differs from what you would normally do.

What have you got to lose? Nothing! Even if you find that this new experience is not for you in the long run, you will have nevertheless learned something which broadens your horizon. Get out of that groove of every-day life and create some excitement by exploring possibilities that lie off the beaten track. You will see, it works!

7. HAPPY SINGLES AND HOW THEY DO IT

WHEN I started writing this book, I began to look for people who could be possible candidates for this last chapter. I asked amongst my friends and told them to look out for me and let me know when they spotted a happy single amongst their acquaintances.

Luck seemed to be on my side. Within the first few weeks I had a dozen candidates who, according to their friends, were 'ideal'. I got in touch with a few of them and they agreed to give me an interview once I got to the last chapter.

Half a year later, I was ready for the last chapter and started ringing around. Out of twelve possibles, two had got married, four had started going out with someone and another four were no longer sure that they were happy. This left me with two who had managed to stay single *and* happy over the previous six months. So the search began again. . . .

The following four interviews have made it into the book because they are all about people who have spent time without a partner, either repeatedly or over a long period of time. Names and professional details have been changed to ensure confidentiality.

VALERIE (50)

Valerie was born in the countryside during the war. After the war, she moved to London with her parents and sister. Here, she went to school and later to college where she got a degree in modern languages.

At the age of 19, she married and had two sons fairly quickly. Before her children were born, she worked in the City as a secretary but stopped work for eleven years to look after the children.

She divorced her husband after 13 years and lived on her own with her children for three years until she met her second husband. They had been married for three years when he had a massive heart attack and died.

While with her second husband, Valerie started studying counselling and therapy work. She is now a full time therapist and also writes books.

VP: Valerie, how long have you been on your own?

V: Nine years, with a gap in the middle of about 18 months when I lived with somebody.

VP: So at the moment, looking back, you've been on your own for six years?

V: Yes.

VP: Tell me, why do you consider yourself a happy single? What makes it so enjoyable?

V: I love being on my own. I love living on my own. I can do what I want *when* I want. I can be with people if I want to be, I can be alone if I want to be. Eat when I want to, paint my toenails if I want to, go to bed when I want to, go out whenever I want to. It's selfish but I enjoy the fact that there's no one else to think about.

VP: How do you go about holidays? Lots of singles find that particularly difficult, especially single women.

V: I either go with a friend or sometimes with more than one friend, or I go on a holiday which has a purpose, like a course, and this might be quite a light-hearted one. I never go on holidays where you sit on beaches; I've never liked that sort of holiday.

VP: Have you actually ever been on a holiday on your own which wasn't a hobby holiday?

V: Yes I have. It was touring in Southern Ireland.

VP: And how did you get on?

V: Fine, because I went to the places I wanted to see and I stopped when I wanted to. I tended to stay at motels and country hotels rather than big hotels. In the evenings, I would sit and talk quite happily to whoever was there, that's just how I am, and then go on my way again the next day, and that was great.

VP: Now tell me one thing – the classic situation for single people is that horrible time when you've got to go down to dinner by yourself, you've got to sit down and eat the meal by yourself. How do you deal with that?

V: I think maybe that is the reason why I stayed at country hotels rather than posh plastic modern hotels where I might have felt more awkward. In country hotels it is more informal, people from other tables talk to each other, so it didn't worry me in the slightest.

VP: Have you always been like that?

V: Yes, my mother always used to tell me that I'd get into trouble for talking to people in bus queues. It's never worried me. At 17 I travelled around Sweden on my own for six months.

VP: So that's just your nature?

V: That's just me. I don't mind at all.

VP: What advice would you give to somebody who is a new single and who finds these things difficult?

V: Most people, even if they are single, male or female, have friends of some sort. And if you feel really worried about going away on your own, go with a friend. These days it's not unusual to be a single woman or a single man, so there are plenty of other single people around.

VP: When you think about the time when you were first single, what was that like?

V: Because of circumstances, it was horrible. The first time when I was divorced was not so bad because I had two children at home. But the second time was terrible because my husband died unexpectedly. When a divorce is coming, or a separation, you know it's coming and, whether you like it or not, you can mentally get ready for it. When it is a bereavement there is no warning. I was very suddenly on my own. Both my sons had left home; one was at college, the other one away at school. I had to move house in order to earn some money, and where I was living at the time wasn't practical. So it was a new home, a new area and entirely on my own. It was very very difficult. The days seemed so long even though I was working. I thought I'd never ever get used to it.

VP: How long did it take you until you were halfway back to normal?

V: It's hard to say because I was getting over the bereavement *and* coping with all the other changes; but within six months it was fine, it was more or less all right again.

VP: Which qualities do you think helped you overcome this difficult situation so quickly?

V: I think it was doing work that I enjoyed. Also, me being me, I got to know people where I was living and then we had school holidays and my sons came to stay and life had a routine again. I think that helps. When you are suddenly in a new place, you don't know where anything is. You don't know which shops are the good ones, you don't know where the post office is, and so on. All your surroundings are new, your way of life is new, everything is new, so the whole thing is strange. Once it all becomes familiar and you get routines going, it becomes much easier.

VP: But don't you think sometimes it may help to be in a different place because then at least things don't remind you of your bereavement?

V: No, I don't think that would make any difference. In fact, for a bereaved person I wouldn't recommend moving away, I don't think it's a good thing. I had to do it just to earn some money, but I don't actually think that it is a good thing.

VP: You think the change is too much to cope with?

V: Yes, because I think you actually need to be
       reminded of things for a while even if it hurts.
       There's the place where he or she sat, or there's
       the cinema where you used to go together. It's sad
       but it's comforting. Also if you have been in a place
       together you've probably made some friends in that
       area who are usually pretty supportive.

VP: What is your attitude towards relationships at this
       point in time?

V: Well, since the time my husband died I've had one
       'live-in' relationship for the best part of two years.
       That was about 18 months after my husband died.
       It didn't work out in the end though we parted
       the best of friends . . . From where I am now I
       don't think I would ever want a live-in relationship
       again.

VP: You feel that the advantages of being single are
       too great?

V: Yes. I'm not anti-men, I enjoy going out with men,
       but I really don't want the hassle of living with
       someone if I don't love them, or the bit that hurts
       if you do. I'm much happier without that.

VP: So how do you see the future in terms of a relation-
       ship?

V: I prefer to think of a loving friendship with some-
       body who I like. I would hate not to have any
       contact or any kind of relationship at all. But I
       would rather not have a relationship than have a
       relationship for the sake of having one. I don't
       think I could ever go out looking for a relationship.
       I'm not into singles clubs and that sort of thing.

VP: What do you think is driving people who do go to
       singles clubs?

V: I think they are actually trying to bolster their own
       ego. Being on your own you either feel, 'I'm on
       my own because I'm me and am a complete person'
       or, 'There must be something wrong with me
       because I'm on my own.' I think that people who
       go looking for another relationship need someone
       to tell them that there is nothing wrong with them.
       I feel that I'm a complete person within myself, so
       I don't need to chase after new relationships. I'm

OK. I'm not perfect, but I'm OK. I don't need someone else to boost my self-esteem.

VP: How about loneliness? Do you get it, and how do you cope with it?

V: I actually don't get it. Neither the fear, nor the loneliness.

VP: Why is that do you think?

V: I think if I were the kind of person that sat at home and had no friends of either sex, then yes, I'd be lonely. But on 'fed-up' days, which we all get, there is always someone I can phone and chat to or go out for a drink with, so I don't actually feel that. Maybe if I were single and had never had a relationship I would feel differently because then I wouldn't know what I was missing out on. Or I might desperately want children and not have had them. But I've done that part, and unless somebody absolutely fantastic comes along and sweeps me off my feet – and I still fancy Paul Newman even though he's old – I can't actually see myself doing anything to go back into another relationship. You get very selfish being on your own. It's lovely. All the decor in my house is to my taste. The food is what I want to eat. If I don't want to eat I don't – I don't have to cook for somebody else. If I go somewhere it's because I want to go there, not because I'm trying to do someone else a favour.

VP: Which qualities in yourself do you think make you so contented with your life?

V: I think it's important to be able to get on with people. A lot of women tend to withdraw into themselves and therefore have nobody they really relate to, man or woman, and I think that must make things very difficult. The longer you go without company the more you are going to worry about it and the more you think there is something wrong with you. But I think that if you are basically content with yourself and you have other people you can call on and you have things which interest you or a job that you like, you are OK.

VP: So basically you are saying that being outgoing and

making contact with other people easily is a quality
in yourself that helps you be happy?

V: I think so. It's one thing being isolated because you
choose to be, but if you are isolated because you
feel there isn't an alternative, that must be horrible.

VP: Is there any advice you would give to someone
who is having problems with being single?

V: I think if you don't feel you can do anything else,
try joining something. It doesn't have to be a club.
Try joining an evening class where there are people
interested in the same things as you. *Don't* go there
to look for a partner, just look for people who have
interests in common with you. If you are shy, then
you can't just go to a dance and walk up and talk
to people. But if you are all learning Italian then
you've got something to talk about, there are coffee
breaks and you get to know people and there will
probably be one that you will get to know outside
the class. It all comes down to thinking that you
matter, and so many people don't think they do.

PETER (23)

Peter comes from the north of England and now works
in sales in London.

When he first moved down, he did not know anyone,
and that was a time he found very difficult because, as
he remarked, London can be quite oppressive when you
are on your own.

Peter has been in quite a few jobs since he left school.
He is now working in sales which he enjoys because it
provides variety and entails dealing with people. He has
just broken off with his girlfriend.

VP: Peter, how long have you been single?

P: About three weeks.

VP: Have there been times before when you have been
on your own? And what has been the longest time
you have spent alone?

P: You mean between relationships? . . . About eighteen months.

VP: It's not very long ago that you split up, so it must still be a bit difficult. How are you coping?

P: Well, it was my decision. It had been on the cards for a long time.

VP: How long did this last relationship go on for?

P: Just over two years.

VP: What are your plans for the future? How are you living at the moment?

P: Same as I ever was. Nothing has changed except that I don't see my girlfriend. I still go out.

VP: What is your social life like then?

P: Monday to Thursday non-existent – I'm just too tired during the week, but I make sure I go out at weekends.

VP: Tell me a bit about your social life.

P: I like music; I like going to see bands and going to pubs. There's a pub I'm rather fond of where they have a lot of comedy on, and I know them all down there.

VP: When you were single before, did you ever go on holiday alone?

P: I've been on holiday without a girlfriend but not on my own.

VP: So if you go, who do you go with?

P: Friends.

VP: And what type of holiday do you go on?

P: I have been to Amsterdam, Ireland, places like that. I like interesting holidays, not just a beach. I like somewhere different where you can go and explore.

VP: So what do you actually do on your holidays?

P: Just do the same sort of thing you do at home, only you're doing it in a different place. So it's new places, new faces, and just let it soak in.

VP: How about eating on your own?

P: I couldn't do it! It amazes me when I go into a restaurant and see people eating alone because it is something I wouldn't do. I'd rather cook at home for myself.

VP: What's the thing about it that you find so impossible?

P: Eating is great and it's a good time for talking, like

after dinner conversations, for example. You can't
do that on your own, can you.

VP: No, that's true. So, tell me, how do you deal with
feelings when you don't feel too good, when you
have had a lousy day at the office, for example?

P: I throw myself into a book. When I'm in a bad
mood I like to be alone. I like a lot of time to
myself for my own thoughts and to do my own
thing. I love reading, you just get lost in a book.
It takes you to another place you can just forget
about everything. After a couple of hours I'm OK
again. Life's too short to be down. I could walk
out of here and get knocked down by a taxi, and
what's the use of being knocked over by a taxi
when you're miserable? You might as well go with
a smile on your face. That's the way I look at it.
I'm definitely an optimist.

VP: How do you see the future? Are you thinking about
another relationship or is that the furthest thing
from your mind at the moment?

P: It's not the furthest thing from my mind at the
moment, but you just don't know what's going to
happen; I mean, I could leave here and meet someone at the bus stop or wherever and it could spark
up. That's how I met my last girlfriend. It was pure
coincidence. I don't go looking for it, I don't go
thinking, 'God, I haven't got anybody.' It will
happen. It will. I'm not actively seeking it or not
seeking it.

VP: Does it cause any problems that you are single
when you are going out with your friends and they
are all couples?

P: With my friends, I don't think that matters so much
any more. But if you're going out to a dinner party
for example, then yes, but if you are going to the
pub or a party it doesn't matter. It's a positive boon
going to a party if you're single.

VP: And why is that?

P: You've not got to worry about the other person.
You're on your own, you can be yourself. I found
sometimes when I was with my girlfriend I was
trying to be somebody that I wasn't. Whereas when

you go on your own, people take you as they find
you.

VP: So in a way it's more relaxed for you?

P: Definitely.

VP: What other advantages do you find it has being on
your own rather than being with somebody else?

P: For one thing, it's cheaper, believe me! *And* you've
just got no restrictions, you can come and go and
do as you will and that's how I like to do it. I've
got nobody expecting me to do things and be there,
apart from myself, so I can do what I want.

VP: What personal qualities do you think you have that
help you to be a happy single?

P: I like my own company. I like time on my own,
whether it's twenty minutes, three weeks or two
seconds.

VP: But when you say time on your own, you don't
mean not seeing your friends, do you?

P: There are times when I don't want to see anybody
– when I've had a really awful day or something's
really got on top of me. I really need to be alone
then, and it does not bother me in the least. But
otherwise, I still need my friends, I'd be lost without them.

VP: What advice would you give to somebody who sits
at home and is utterly unhappy being single?

P: Get out there and do something about it! You are
not going to meet anybody sitting at home. You've
got to go out, find places where you can meet
people with a similar sort of outlook on life as you.
You only get out of it what you put into it. It's a
big world, there are a lot of people out there and
anything can happen. Don't go out and expect to
find somebody; just have a good time. You've got
to be an optimist, because you can't go round with
a long face on. When I'm not feeling too good, I
try to make other people laugh. Hopefully it'll raise
a smile and that brings me out of it.

VP: How important is your job in your life?

P: It's pretty important, though it's not the be all and
end all. In my present job I'm working with people
which I love. I get a chance to talk to people all

day and it's great, I enjoy it. I like variety, it's the spice of life, and I certainly get that in this job.

NATALIE (43)

Natalie works for a university as a systems analyst. She is self-employed.

Natalie met Tony when she was 18. At the age of 23, she moved in with him and they spent the next 15 years together. When the relationship grew stale, they decided to separate. This turned out to be a long-drawn process, partly because they had been together for so long and partly because they had had a nice life-style together which they were reluctant to abandon. In the end, it took three years to accomplish the separation.

VP: How long have you been single?

N: Five years.

VP: How come that you cope with being on your own when lots of people, especially women, feel really unhappy about it?

N: I think I've always been a loner. Whenever I was with someone, to a certain degree I resented being with them all the time. So when I was finally by myself, I enjoyed myself thoroughly. Even after the novelty wore off, I still liked it.

VP: You call yourself a loner. Have you therefore decided that relationships are too much hassle?

N: I don't think they are too much hassle; it's just that I've not found anyone I'd like to have a relationship with. I haven't found anyone that I'd remotely want to be with.

VP: Not even remotely? That bad, is it?

N: It's that bad. I've never found anyone for whom I've felt 'this is it'. In four years of 'playing the field', having dates, I've never got past first base really.

VP: What is second base then?

N: It's finding someone who is, I suppose, like me. Someone who likes what I want to do, who is not so oriented towards money. I'm not prepared to go with just anyone; they've got to meet certain criteria. I'm too long in the tooth now for the social ladder climbing and everything that goes with it. I don't want any of that. I did meet someone who I thought was just right, but he was married, so it was a no-no. And in four years he's the only one for whom I could say, 'I will go with him wherever.'

VP: You seem to have more or less decided that it is very unlikely that you will find anybody. How does that make you feel?

N: OK. I was so relieved after that last relationship to be by myself. Sometimes on a weekend I look around me and think, 'What am I going to do?' and it's like a high – I can do what I like. I still get that feeling, it hasn't passed after five years!

VP: What do you do about holidays?

N: I can quite easily go on my own but I don't so much any more; I go with friends. In June I shall be taking my niece away with me. Later I shall be visiting Turkey with four other women. In August I'm going to Tuscany for two weeks with a woman and a man, both single. With different people, never with the same people.

VP: What do you think is the advantage of going with other people rather than on your own?

N: Companionship is one advantage, because the people I go away with I *choose* to go with, and I usually find they like the same type of things that I like.

VP: Would you say it's more fun to go with other people or is it just as much fun going on your own?

N: I could quite easily go on my own; this has never been a problem.

VP: How do you deal with things like eating out alone?

N: I suppose the standard thing is to have a book there so that if anyone bothers you you can start reading and it's obvious that you don't want to know. But I've always found that going on holiday by myself I usually eat in the hotel restaurant for

the first few days. Then people know you are by
yourself and make conversation. I find I actually
meet more people when I'm on my own. If you are
fairly open and friendly, it's never really a problem.

VP: Will you approach people when you are alone or
do you find people will approach you?

N: I've always found people have approached me. I've
never gone out of my way to approach other
people, because if they don't then that's fine, I can
sit and read a book or go for a walk or something
else. I've never found that to be a problem. In my
experience, people will ask me eventually to join
them. I don't know whether they feel sorry for me,
I hope I've never given that impression!

VP: Well, you certainly don't sound like you feel sorry
for yourself.

N: Oh no!

VP: Can you tell me how your professional life ties in
with you being single? Does it make a difference
to you that you are self-employed?

N: Yes, definitely, because I like the feeling of being
a free agent. I like to feel that I am independent.
I am independent in a lot of ways, much more
than a lot of people. I don't have the restrictions,
and that has helped me a good deal.

VP: Does it ever happen to you that you do feel a bit
lonely?

N: Yes. The times that it hits me are when I am with
my sister's family – she has four children. She has
an ongoing life and she knows what will happen
in the next ten years, that her daughters will marry,
etc. This family unity is an ongoing thing which I
don't have, and sometimes I regret that, but not
very often.

VP: So how do you deal with these occasional pangs
of regret?

N: The regret is there but there's nothing I can do
about it, and I'm an optimist so I carry on. It's
there, then it goes, and finito, until the next time
around.

VP: What would you say the qualities are that you need
to be a happy single?

N: It helps if you like your own company. I also think
      it helps sometimes to have a good imagination.
      Alone you can imagine much more than when you
      are with someone else. For example, you can
      imagine perhaps that you are somewhere, that you
      have an aim, and there is every chance that it can
      come true because it's up to you to get there.
      Whereas when you are with someone you have to
      consider that person, as well as any children you
      may have if you are a family, and that makes it
      less likely that you will achieve your aim. I always
      think to myself that there could be something
      better around the corner and I am free to grab it.
      I am not restricted, I can still do it if I want to.
      The resentment in the relationship was that I
      couldn't do what I wanted a lot of the time, there
      was always something that held me back, i.e. him.
      I feel that now, on my own, I'm my own person.
      In the relationship, I was who he wanted me to
      be.

RUPERT (36)

Rupert comes from rather an extraordinary background.
He spent eight years as an officer in the military service,
in particular in the SAS. After his time there had come
to an end, he attended university and got an MBA.

At the age of twenty-nine he was diagnosed as having
cancer and was given six months to live. He argued
vigorously with the medical profession and set out to
prove them wrong – and did.

He then started working in corporate finance, advanc-
ing rapidly into senior positions until he got to the top
of the ladder as managing director. When he realized
that he could not get any higher, he started his own
business.

Rupert's last relationship goes back two years.

VP: Rupert, you volunteered to be interviewed on the
      topic of happy singles. What makes you one? What
      is the recipe?

R: I think it's that I'm satisfied with my lot. Life is full, it is going in a positive direction, I'm successful on the professional front, and I'm single by choice.

VP: I know you are very busy running your business. Do you get any time for holidays?

R: I make a point of taking a holiday of one or two weeks at least every three months. I will go to stay with friends or go away with friends. I will not generally go on holiday by myself because I have lots of people to go with.

VP: But have you actually ever tried to go on holiday by yourself?

R: Oh yes, I have. I have travelled the world by myself. I quite enjoyed it. The art of being by yourself is knowing how to get to know other people, and I always managed to do that.

VP: Do you approach other people or do you wait for them to come to you?

R: I'm rather a shy person, so I wouldn't make the first move, but by doing activities, like climbing or canoeing for example, you meet other people and share the adventure with them. Just because you are single does not imply that you are divorced from others. You've just got to go and arrange these activities and do it!

VP: Would you generally recommend to singles to go on activity holidays rather than beach holidays?

R: No. Beach holidays can be great fun, too. Take the Club Med. That's a beach holiday, but with lots of things to do. Everything is arranged for you, and there is no problem getting to know people.

VP: What about your free time at home? Does that involve friends or will you sometimes go out and eat by yourself?

R: I frequently eat out by myself, and I quite enjoy my own company in doing so. I don't even have to hide behind a book like so many people have to.

VP: So as you are sitting in a restaurant by yourself, what do you assume other people think about you?

R: I don't know . . . I'm not really conscious of other people there, but I certainly don't expect them to consider me an oddball. I just go into a restaurant to enjoy the food and a nice bottle of wine, and if people think anything about me it's probably, 'Why is he so happy?'

VP: How about other activities outside work, besides eating?

R: I make a conscious effort to get out of the house. What I enjoy doing is running. There are some wonderful runs around the park next door and the woods, and I normally take an hour and a half or two hours every day. That's one way of getting out.

I think that if you want to be a very successful single person you have to be organized. I'm not that well organized, I never plan that far in advance what I'll be doing on a certain evening. So a lot of the time I end up being by myself at night time. It doesn't worry me though; I always find something to do.

VP: How important are your friends in your life?

R: Very important. I have a small number of friends, but they are *true* friends, not just acquaintances. They are really a surrogate for having a partner. There is one friendship in particular which I find very satisfying, and this is with a female friend of mine who is married abroad. I can share everything with her, talk to her about everything, and this provides the emotional support that I need as a single person. So we are on the phone to one another a lot, and I enjoy that enormously.

VP: But it's not a so-called 'intimate' relationship in the physical sense?

R: No, it isn't.

VP: Have there been such relationships in the past?

R: Yes, there have been a few, but all of them fairly short-term. My last relationship ended two years ago, and that had only been going on for about six months.

I think that there are only one or two women in the world who are right for me, and I'd rather wait for the right person than go crazy about not having a partner.

VP: That sounds like a very relaxed attitude. Tell me,

what role does your work play in your life as a
single?

R: It is very important to me because it is a challenge
to run your own business, and because the money
I'm making enables me to do what I want. I have
made a commitment to myself that I'll work really
hard until I'm 40 and then live off the proceeds,
take time off and go travelling around the world,
meeting up with old friends and so on.

VP: So work has two positive sides to it – you enjoy
doing it in the first place and it provides you with
the money you need to pursue your other interests.

R: Yes, absolutely.

VP: You sound a very positive and determined person.
How do you do it?

R: I think you've got to have your values resolved.
You've got to understand what life is all about and
have a view of why you exist. After three years of
intense research and exploring the spiritual side of
life, I've come to the conclusion that it's all about
personal growth. My beliefs focus on the concept
of reincarnation, even though, basically, I'm not a
religious person. But I think that each life is about
becoming better and learning more about yourself
and to interrelate with others.

The most important quality I see is being at peace
with yourself and going your own way, and that
may not be the conventional way of marrying and
having children.

When I look at my life so far, I can say that I
have had quite a few unique experiences. After my
time in the military I went for an MBA at university
and then I found out that I had cancer. At the time
I lived with my mother who looked after me during
my illness. I had already decided to fight the cancer
with everything I had got, despite gloomy predic-
tions from the medical profession. I was determined to win the battle, so when my mother gave
me breakfast in the mornings with tears rolling
down her cheeks every time, I decided I had to
leave. I didn't want to be influenced by her misery.
I left and radically changed my lifestyle for the

next six months, living on raw vegetables and water only – and the next scan showed no trace of cancer whatsoever.

I think it's really very important to associate yourself with positive people, because they can push you forward and make you happy. Don't hang out with low achievers and listen to their moans and groans! If you do, you'll join them eventually.

Life is all about building up a range of experiences that allow you to grow personally, and I cannot emphasize enough the power of positive thinking. You've got to have good, close friends, you have to have confidence in yourself and you've got to go for it. You get out of life what you put into it.

ABILITIES AND SKILLS THAT HELP

When we look at the above interviews, there are some characteristics that stand out as being particularly useful when you are without a partner.

There is no doubt that you need to be considerably more active on your own than when you are with someone else. As you have seen, those interviewed often choose friends to accompany them on holidays or weekends away, and this is certainly a good way of taking a lot of the pressure off you. Sharing an experience with someone else is in itself entertaining, so even if you go for a rather mundane outing, say for example a visit to your local pub, it is fun because the other person brings with them their views and opinions and experiences – and comments about the quality of the beer in your local or the hairstyle of the bloke in the corner. . . .

It is a fact that often outings can be more fun with friends than they are with a partner. The reason for this is that you can be yourself more with friends. They accept you as you are, whereas your partner has certain expectations of you. You can't just go to the theatre in your jeans, you have to wear some 'nice' clothes; you can't just knock up a quick lunch, you have to go and buy serviettes because his colleague from work is coming over; and so on. Friends, on the other hand, just take you as they find you, and that makes the whole enterprise more relaxed.

Alone or with friends, let us have a look at the qualities you need to get your life as a soloist on to the right tracks.

LIKING YOUR OWN COMPANY

This is probably the greatest asset that you can have as a single. Feeling contented when you are on your own means that you are at peace with yourself, that you can accept yourself with all your strengths and weaknesses and that, when it comes to the crunch and you spend that weekend all by yourself, you are still having a good time.

The problem with spending time in your own company is that it allows you to *think*. This is fine as long as you like yourself; it is pretty unpleasant, however, if you have unfinished business on the emotional front. When you feel incompetent or a failure in any respect you will experience these negative emotions so much more strongly when there are no distractions. As we have seen in Chapter 5, the party-goer and the career person make sure they avoid any confrontations with their own shortcomings by throwing themselves into their social life or their work.

You can quite easily find out whether there is any unfinished business lurking in the depths of your subconscious mind. All you need to do is to sit down for ten minutes; no radio, no television, no book or magazine or paper. Just sit there. Now see what thoughts come into your mind. Are they pleasant? Are they disturbing? You may be surprised how long ten minutes are when you are alone with your thoughts. . . .

If you have problems with being by yourself, concentrate on Chapter 6, pp 79 ff and pp 106 ff.

BEING OUTGOING

All four interviewees emphasized the importance of being part of a social network. Although they all liked their own company, they nevertheless felt that this needed to be counterbalanced by having company.

The intensity and closeness of friendships people maintain varies, of course. There can be quite a wide spectrum, ranging from acquaintances to pals to bosom friends, but they are all needed to give colour to your life.

The need to maintain a good social life will naturally involve you making certain efforts towards it. As Peter said after his interview, 'It's no good sitting at home, waiting for someone to knock on your door. You'll have to go out there and show your face, go to places where you meet people, or they won't know you exist!'

Being outgoing doesn't mean you have to go and chat up others. Both Natalie and Rupert said in their interviews that they don't actually approach others when they are on holiday, but they are open to being talked to. Being outgoing, therefore, can also mean an open attitude towards being contacted, and this can, for example, come across by you allowing eye contact, greeting people you have seen before and smiling as a sign of recognition. These are all 'openers' that will allow others to approach you without you forcing yourself on them.

If you want to be slightly more active you can pick up a cue from the other person. If you see them carrying a book, you can use this as an opener by asking them about it. Depending how things go, you may get into a conversation and take it from there, or, if you don't enjoy it, you can get out of it quite gracefully by leaving once your question has been answered.

What have you got to lose by trying it? Only your own fear. The risks you are taking are smaller than you may think, and the gains can be considerable. You may get half an hour's pleasant conversation out of it, or a companion for your holiday, or a good friend.

Expect the half-hour chat, and let everything else be a bonus, and you can't go wrong.

If you have problems with this area, concentrate on Chapter 6, pp 87 ff and pp 95 ff.

HAVING A JOB YOU ENJOY

Another point on which all interviewees agreed was that, since you spend a considerable number of hours a week at work, you might as well make sure you choose something you enjoy.

This of course is not as easy as it sounds. Arriving at the final decision of what is the right job is often a matter of hit and miss. Before you can say whether you like a job you have to try it out, and this takes time. There are few people who have a vocation which they can follow from day one. Most people have to undergo a process of personal development over the years until they arrive at a point in their life where they are sure what it is they want to do professionally, even though an underlying theme may have been visible from early on. Peter said that, except for one disastrous exception in an office job, he has always looked for people-orientated work. Rupert has always aspired to be the leader in whatever he did. On the other hand, Valerie's decision to work as a therapist took a long time to evolve, simply because she was distracted from a career by being a mother and having to bring up two children single-handed after her divorce.

When a particular talent is apparent in a person, their professional path is more obvious than for someone who is either not aware of their talent or has no particular leaning towards a specific area of interest. Whatever your own situation, it is worth spending time on assessing your potential and your possibilities. I sincerely believe that the best choice is always to do what comes easiest to you. (No, I'm afraid there is not yet anything like a professional money-spender on the job market.)

Work should be satisfying, interesting and fun, and it should feel natural to you. Of course, no job can be all these things all of the time, but you can certainly look for something that fulfils most of these criteria most of the time. Once you start looking, you are already halfway there.

Think back to what you wanted to become when you were little. Often, these childhood dreams give us pointers as to our inclinations. As Natalie said in her interview, you need imagination in order to achieve your aims in life; in other words, we have to see a goal clearly in our mind's eye so that it can be achieved, and that is something children are very good at. They *play* at being a teacher because they *see* themselves as one in their imagination. Charles Forte used to play 'hotel' as a child, and look how well that's worked for him!

Spend some time mulling over what you want to do with the rest of your professional life. If you are happy with what you are doing, that's great. If you are not, change it. You will find help with how to achieve this in Chapter 6, pp 117 ff.

BEING ENTERPRISING

An enterprise is an event which launches you into the great unknown, into an area which lies outside the radius of experiences that you have had to date. We all need a certain amount of this spirit in order to progress and develop our true potential.

Playing it safe all the time has one big disadvantage – it is boring. Subsequently you get phlegmatic, and, worst of all, you get boring. In order to get some sparkle back into your life you will have to take certain risks. These risks don't need to be big. They can simply consist of trying out something new, something that is unusual for you. Buy a different newspaper; change to a different radio station; spend some time listening to classical music instead of pop. Successful singles undertake new ventures every once in a while.

Out of the four people interviewed for this book, three are self-employed. This is just another way of being enterprising, this time in a professional sense. It goes without saying that you can be equally happy in a job where you are working for someone else, as is shown in Peter's case. Peter is enterprising within his work. He has chosen a job which is livened up through the variety of people and situations he has to deal with during the day. This constitutes a challenge which keeps him interested in what he is doing. In the self-employed group, Natalie takes pleasure from the fact that she is her own boss, working more or less the hours and days she chooses. Valerie enjoys the challenge of helping her patients find better ways of dealing with their lives, and in the process of doing so, she has to be flexible and inventive; Rupert is intent on building up his business, expanding it and diversifying it to its maximum capacity, with the aim of (so he assures me) becoming amazingly rich in the process.

All four of them have one thing in common – they are actively seeking to promote their own happiness. They are motivated to reach their aims, and they are clear about what these aims are.

If you feel that you need to work on this area, re-read Chapter 6, pp 115 ff.

THINKING POSITIVELY

All four interviews feature one predominant character-istic, and that is optimism. The interviewees expect life to be interesting and rewarding, they expect good times to be just round the corner. Rupert in particular showed how powerful positive thinking is, especially in times when you seem to have little reason to be optimistic.

Thinking positively does not mean that you only see things through rose-tinted spectacles or that you are in a good mood all the time. It would be foolish to expect that you can live your life without encountering obstacles and problems. There is nothing you can do about certain things going wrong, but you can certainly do something about the way you handle these events. By putting your-self into a positive frame of mind, you will feel better within yourself and you will, therefore, cope better with the problematic situations. The techniques of how to achieve this positive outlook are described in detail in *Positive Thinking*.

It may appear that Natalie, Peter, Valerie and Rupert are all 'naturals', but you don't have to be – this is something that can be learned along the way. Valerie appears to have an innate positive disposition judging from her memories of 'always talking to people in bus queues', happily expecting to have an interesting conversation with someone. Peter appears to have picked up the ability as he went along. He told me in the interview that he used to be overweight when he was at school and got teased for it a lot. It bothered him for quite a while, until one day he decided he was no longer prepared to be bothered by it. He adopted the attitude that people would just have to like him as he was if they wanted to be his friends. Having decided on this approach he got rid of his unease – and quite a few pounds.

Some people are born with it, others pick it up along the way. If you are not a natural, don't despair – being optimistic is something you can learn, just like swimming, dancing or riding a bike. It is worth acquiring this skill because it will make you feel happier. As a consequence, other people will feel more comfortable with you, and everyone will have a much better time for it.

If you find it a struggle to be optimistic, concentrate on Chapter 6, pp 79 ff or delve into my other book about positive thinking.

STOP BEING SENSIBLE ALL THE TIME!

HAVE FUN!

PUT MAGIC INTO YOUR LIFE!

INDEX